MW01633673

Other books in the series

Of Peats and Putts – A whisky and golf tour of Scotland

Mashies and Mash-Tuns –
A whisky and golf tour of England, Wales and Ireland

Of Peats and Putts Continental -
Exploring Whisky and Golf across Europe

OF PEATS AND PUTTS
THE BACK 9

A NEW WHISKY AND GOLF TOUR OF SCOTLAND

ANDREW BROWN

YOUCAXTON
PUBLICATIONS

Contents

Preface

'L'accent du pays ou l'on est né demeure dans l'esprit
et dans le coeur, comme dans le langage'
'The accent of one's birthplace lingers in the mind
and in the heart as it does in one's speech'

François de la Rochefoucauld 1613-1680
French author and moralist

SCOTLAND, THE LAND of my birth and my childhood, still has a pull on me. *'Will ye no come back again'*, the famous Jacobite lament, is perhaps more apt than the maxim of Rochefoucauld. I had always planned to return to Scotland, as I felt that my first book left out so many whisky and golfing gems. I have, since writing it, been exploring how golf and whisky have travelled outside the land of their invention, with my second book exploring the rest of the United Kingdom and Ireland and the third, Europe. This has helped broaden my perspective and will I hope contribute to interpreting developments within Scotland. There certainly have been many of these as the number of new distilleries in Scotland increases every year; since I finished *Of Peats and Putts* in late 2017, there have been, by my calculation, over twenty new openings and there are at time of writing many more in the pipeline. It is not the same story with golf courses where the supply and demand equation is quite different and I can point to just two new courses of note opening in that time-period while a couple of major projects have not come to fruition. Perhaps the most notable new one in prospect is the planned second course at Castle Stuart.

Having considered this second book on Scotland, I have also come to decision. While choosing nine locations for my first book was difficult, choosing another nine to complete the eighteen was even more problematic to the extent that I have decided that there will be a third book – *Of Peats and Putts* will become a trilogy; in golfing terminology a 27-hole complex and in whisky parlance there will be three expressions. Those of you who understand me will realise that golfing locations which use the word 'complex' are not usually my favourite. No, *Of Peats and Putts* will have three nines; I'm thinking here of the likes of Portmarnock or St George's Hill. '*The back 9*' here will geographically be biased to the east, while my third nine will hug the west coast and finish up in Orkney. The third nine will also have its own very specific identity both in golfing and whisky terms; more about that later.

The development of the Scotch whisky industry is remarkable whether you look at a perspective of two-hundred years, a hundred years, fifty years or just the past five years. A simplistic review of industry history would point to a number of key periods; the two-hundred year perspective takes us back to the 1823 Excise Act which enabled commercial distilling to prosper; the late 19th century saw, following the invention of the patent-still process, the emergence of Blended Scotch which saw the Scottish industry overtake the Irish and put it in a much stronger position to survive the twin shocks of the Great War and US Prohibition; the beginnings of the Single

Malt revolution started slowly in the 1960s and again enabled the industry to survive the 1970s downturn; and, finally, the dramatic number of new distillery openings and old distillery investment and re-openings which have characterised the early years of this century. I still find it remarkable how young the Single Malt market is. In Professor David Daiches' seminal book, *Scotch Whisky, Its Past and Present*, first published in 1969, he notes that the big Scotch blended brands liked to promote their heritage and the traditional pot-still malt whisky process while refusing to declare the proportions of malt and mass-produced grain whisky in their various products. He observes that 'the proportion of single malts to blends consumed is very small; but there is nevertheless a steady rise in the availability and the consumption of single malts both in Britain and certain overseas countries' while noting that 'few single malts are advertised'. At that time, single malts represented a tiny percentage of the market; today, measured in exports, Single Malt Scotch (I use capital letters here as it has since become a formal term as defined in the Scotch Whisky Regulations of 2009) accounts for just 11% of sales volume though over one third of sales value. This clearly points to the future; while many trends will point to a reduction in global alcohol consumption there is opportunity for premium, high value products. I will consider these trends as I visit the various distilleries.

While most of the distilleries I have visited for this leg of the tour were new to me, many of the golf courses I had played before. Many people have a bucket list of golf courses they plan to play, for example: the Top 100 in a particular country, all the Open venues, all the links courses in Scotland. I have a friend who has played all the 'Royal' courses in the United

Kingdom and all the clubs that have hosted the Ryder, Walker, Solheim and Curtis Cups. This is fun but I also recommend going back to play courses at least a second time as playing a particular course just once is really not enough to understand it properly. It is like meeting someone for the first time; you will form an impression and you may, or may not, take a liking to them. Only on further acquaintance can you genuinely have a considered view. If someone asks me about my favourite courses, I will only name those that I have played at least twice. There are many courses which I have hugely enjoyed but only played once and therefore yearn to play again as much as notching up another new one. Therefore as well as having a list of courses I want to play for the first time, I keep a bucket list of those I want to play again. I think the same is likely to be true about visiting distilleries; it is certainly true about tasting whisky. I need to have had a few drams on different occasions to be able pass a fair judgement.

So, join me as I start on the 'Black Isle' (famously, it is neither black nor an isle) and make my way via Speyside, Aberdeenshire, Perthshire, Fife and Edinburgh to finish in my childhood home, the Scottish Borders. I will include a mix of the famous (Glenfiddich and Cruden Bay) and the less famous (Glen Ord and Hopeman) as well as the old (Glenturret and Musselburgh) and the new (Lindores Abbey and The Roxburghe). For the third nine, I will start in Dumfries and Galloway and head up the west coast via Arran, Islay, Skye, the Outer Hebrides, Sutherland and Caithness to end up on Orkney. These two 'nines' have very different characteristics; the golf courses on the eastern nine are higher rated (seven of the nine are rated in the Top 100 in Scotland while on the western nine only two are) and while the eastern nine includes a mix of older and new distilleries, the western will focus, though not quite exclusively, on start-ups.

While I will describe the courses and distilleries which I visit and look to put them in the context of developments in golf and whisky, you will not escape my further musings on a variety of subjects. There is always more musing to be done on both whisky and golf. Prepare then, during the course of these two books, for discussions about slow play (which I still dislike) and the problem with the ball being hit endlessly further (which I still feel needs addressing). I will again encourage you to play more foursomes golf which I enjoy so much. In whisky I will suggest that the global and the local are now connected and marvel at the prices being paid for some whiskies. And increasingly I will introduce you to the people who sustain these two great Scottish gifts to the world.

I have described before how context is all in the appreciation of both golf and whisky; how the environment is so much a part of the varied experience of both. Yet, I will continue to seek some eternal truths amidst the contextual noise. My third book on Europe was heavily impacted by the distractions of the Brexit process and Covid 19. As we emerge from these, perhaps we can learn some lessons from both which are relevant. While for me the enjoyment of whisky and golf can offer an escape from some of life's harsh realities, neither are immune from global trends and both offer solutions. If environmental change is a major challenge for mankind, so too is it for golf courses. The erosion threatening Montrose, one of Scotland's oldest links, brings that to life, and golf course designers now understand the need to build and design courses in a manner that requires less intervention. In whisky, new start-ups are becoming ever conscious of their carbon footprint and we will see examples of how entrepreneurs are tackling this.

Globalism is another trend which impacts both. Much of the strength of golf in Scotland is the link between golf clubs and their local communities with golf-club membership, for the most part, still being relatively affordable and open to all. Covid 19 also seems to have reversed a trend of declining golf-club membership which is positive. The Scotch whisky industry is booming on the back of globalism with the growth of an aspirant middle class in emerging economies driving increased whisky consumption around the world with Scotch benefiting from its positioning as the original and the best. At the same time, global trade can be a nasty confrontational business, as the tariff disputes between the EU and the US have shown. These can quite quickly have a devasting impact on whisky businesses. The global demand for premium malts has also driven growth in whisky fraud – yes, you sometimes need to check the provenance of that bottle which purports to be a fifty-year-old Single Malt.

All these issues will be discussed, if not examined in detail, because as I have said before, I am better at raising issues than solving them, though I will continue to give my personal perspective on things I feel strongly about. Finally, and more positively, whatever the political, social and economic context, I will seek to demonstrate how the complexities and mysteries intrinsically embedded within the playing of golf and the making of whisky give them both universal and eternal appeal.

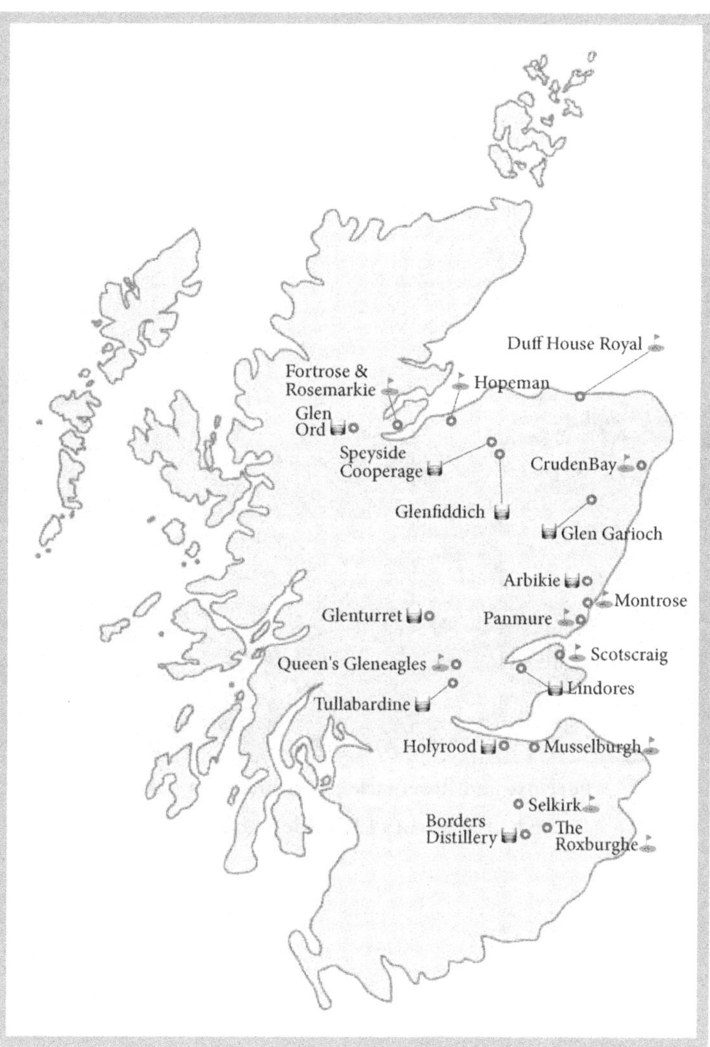

Duff House Royal
Fortrose &
Rosemarkie
Hopeman
Glen
Ord
Speyside
Cooperage
CrudenBay
Glenfiddich
Glen Garioch
Arbikie
Montrose
Glenturret
Panmure
Queen's Gleneagles
Scotscraig
Lindores
Tullabardine
Holyrood
Musselburgh
Selkirk
Borders
Distillery
The
Roxburghe

Fortrose and Rosemarkie is proud of its claim
to be the world's 15th oldest golf club

CHAPTER ONE

THE BLACK ISLE

'We borrowed golf from Scotland as we borrowed whisky.
Not because it is Scottish but because it is good'

Horace Hutchison 1859-1932
English amateur golfer

THE BLACK ISLE is less than an hour south of where I started my original book, in Brora. It is a short drive from Inverness over the distinctive-looking Kessock Bridge which since 1982 has spanned the Beauly Firth. The A9 continues north and to find our whisky we need to turn off to the west and for the golf to the east. There is a symmetry with the first chapter of my first book; the course I have chosen was designed by James Braid, as was Brora, and the distillery is owned by Diageo, as is Clynelish. Until recently all the Highland distilleries in this area were owned by multinational companies; Glenmorangie (LMVH), Balblair (Inver House), Dalmore (Whyte & Mackay), Teaninich and Glen Ord (Diageo). However, there has now been considerable start-up activity with a very small distillery being opened in the Castle Hotel in Dornoch, a slightly bigger one, Glen Wyvis, just outside Dingwall, and a bigger one still, Ardross at Alness which will have a capacity of 1,000,000 litres of pure alcohol. While this is relatively big for a start-up, Glen Ord, the first distillery which we will visit is over ten times that size.

Let's start with the golf, so shortly after the bridge turn east onto the Black Isle. It was once covered in dense woodland which gave it a 'black' appearance. Today it remains sparsely populated, mainly agricultural land with a few small towns and villages. Fortrose and Rosemarkie are two of these villages, about a mile apart on the south-facing Moray Firth coast and both have history with Fortrose having an old derelict cathedral which did not survive the Reformation and Rosemarkie being a site with Pictish stones.

The golf club takes the name of the two villages and its location is remarkable, the course being squeezed onto a very narrow peninsula which juts out into the Moray Firth with arresting views from the end, Chanonry Point, over to Fort George on the other side. It is a well-known location for spotting dolphins, one of the most northerly places in the world to have a population or a 'pod' of these wonderful mammals. The point also has a stone memorial to the Brahan Seer, a legendary 17th-century Gaelic prophet alleged to have predicted all sorts of events from the Battle of Culloden to North Sea oil! Legend states that he met an untimely and rather unpleasant death at Chanonry Point, burnt in a spiked barrel of tar on the orders of the Countess of Seaforth. Apparently when she asked him to predict the reason why her husband had been delayed on his return from Paris, he gave an answer which she didn't appreciate, suggesting that it was because he had been cavorting with a younger and prettier woman.

I have to admit that the first time that I played Fortrose and Rosemarkie, I was a little disappointed. Perhaps, like St Andrews, it takes a little getting used to. The turf is true links and the land is fairly low lying without any significant dunes though there are plenty of gentle slopes, particularly down the centre. It must certainly have been a design challenge as there is very little space with the strip of land narrowing towards the point and is essentially divided into two with a public road running down the central spine. This inevitably leads to some slightly strange holes and some uninteresting ones. However, I also remember on that first occasion that I played quite badly which never helps. It claims to be the '15th oldest recorded club in the world' as there is plenty of evidence of golf being played at the top end of the peninsula during the 18th century and there is a record of some form of club holding an AGM in July 1793. The first formal 9 holes, however, didn't emerge until relatively late in 1888 with the first clubhouse built in 1895. After the Great War, the course was extended to 18 holes but it was in the early 1930s when some more land out towards Chanonry Point was acquired and James Braid was commissioned to redesign the course. This is broadly today's layout and a new clubhouse was built in 1935. The Second World War intervened and the course was requisitioned and used as a training ground for the preparations for the D Day landings. It was revived soon after the end of the war and, in 1958, the club received a benefaction enabling a larger clubhouse to be built which was further extended in 1977 while in 2020 a new building housing the Pro Shop was built behind the first tee. This has been done in an architecturally sensitive manner and looks good.

The routing is in many ways fairly straightforward: four holes down the eastern shore, a short hole across the bottom, three holes back up the western shoreline followed by the Par 3 9th across the top of the central spine; then three holes down the centre, three holes back up the centre before 16 reverses back once again with 17 and the Par 3 18th taking you back to the clubhouse. The problem with lack of space is most evident on the back 9 with holes 10-15 either side of the central road feeling a little constrained. Far be it for me to be critical of the eminent architect James Braid, but it is perhaps surprising that given the space constraint, the course only has three Par 3s and two of these are over 200 yards. By contrast, there are seven Par 4s under 350 yards off the white tees. I am a great fan of short Par 4s but this is perhaps a few too many. Two of these are actually less than 300 yards. Could not a couple of interesting short Par 3s have replaced some of these? It is perhaps holes 13-16 which epitomise this the most – four successive holes, all short Par 4s, with a total length of just 1200 yards.

Still, there is much to enjoy, especially the task of managing the wind to keep yourself away from the prolific gorse. I last played in April and it certainly looked pretty, though gorse is a challenge for greenkeepers and needs managing. Like many other clubs, Fortrose and Rosemarkie is removing quite a lot of it – I had played at Aldeburgh a couple of weeks previously and it was doing the same. Gorse has a role to play in framing fairways but if it becomes too much of a hazard the fun of the game is lost. The turf here is also classic links with many undulations and unpredictable bounces so a combination of tightly gorse-framed fairways, bouncy conditions and crosswinds (as the peninsula broadly runs north/south, the winds are usually across rather than into or behind) makes control quite a challenge. The greens are good, firm, links greens, some with interesting slopes and borrows. The Par 5 4th comes to mind where there are no easy two putts. The 6th and 11th share a double green in the St. Andrews style. Many are slightly raised thereby requiring accuracy with the approach shot.

One aspect of the course which I liked was something I had not seen before. As I have mentioned previously, my golf game is founded more on instinct than exactitude so I don't carry any distance measurement devices and I always ask at the clubhouse whether there are distance markers on the course. It seems to me a courtesy to visitors for these to be present. I was rather disappointed to visit a well-known club in late 2021 and to be told that there weren't any. The Professional explained that there used to be wooden posts in the rough serving as 150-yard markers to the centre of the green but that they had been removed 'because of Covid'. I am not sure whether I was meant to be impressed by this but I wasn't and politely questioned how removing a wooden post, which does not need to be touched, could in any way protect anyone from catching what for some time had been known to be an airborne virus. He didn't have an answer to this except to say; 'Well, I have sold more course planners'. This made me even less impressed. Anyway, by contrast, Fortrose and Rosemarkie provides discreet coloured discs on the fairway and the reason for mentioning this fairly common practice is that they did them at 125 yards and 175 yards instead of the usual 100 and 150 yards. I decided that this was actually more useful. Also, this information was displayed prominently on the scorecard, something which I would encourage. Occasionally I have forgotten to ask and out on the course have taken a few holes to establish whether the markers were to the middle or the front of the green or indeed whether they were in yards or metres. The difference between 150 yards to the middle and 150 metres to the front can be a lot!

The first three Par 4s down the shore are a fairly gentle opening. The Par 5 4th is a greater test requiring accuracy all the way with a narrow hog's back fairway making even a well-directed shot likely to kick off in any direction. 5 is a charming short Par 3 where a front pin position especially will be a challenge. The three holes up the western shore are more spacious and give an opportunity to open the shoulders. I can't say I enjoyed the 9th – a Par 3 of over 200 yards uphill into a cold east wind. My driver wouldn't have made it so I played it as (another) short Par 4. None of the stretch of four short Par 4s from 13-16 require a driver with anything from a medium iron to a 3-wood likely to be the best choice. The finish is quite tough with 17 requiring an accurate drive to the top of a hill to give you a view of the green attractively located down in a dell. 18 is another 200 yard+ Par 3 into a wind but, with its view of the clubhouse from an elevated tee, it has more character than the 9th. Perhaps I also preferred it as I got my 3 – a full drive to about 20 yards short from where I got up and down. Always a good way to finish a round. Is that why I would always want to return? The clubhouse will also afford you a friendly welcome – the catering is provided independently by the 19th Restaurant which is open to the public all day for breakfast, morning coffee and cakes, lunch and early dinners. This is an increasing trend at golf courses; restaurants and cafés setting up in golf clubhouses to serve not just golfers but also the local community and holidaymakers. There is a holiday park just up from the golf course.

A rather charming story is that Fortrose and Rosemarkie was the birthplace of the famous 'Colonel Bogey March'. It was composed by a bandmaster of the 93rd Highlanders Brigade stationed across the Moray Firth from Chanonry Point at Fort George. Officers at Fort George had honorary membership of the club and the bandmaster, Lieutenant Ricketts, would frequently take a boat across to play with his Colonel. The Colonel would prefer to whistle on the course rather than shout the more conventional 'fore' and this inspired Ricketts, a budding composer who used the name Kenneth J Alford for his compositions, to use the familiar two-note whistle – a descending minor third for those of a musical bent – as the basis for his famous March. 'Bogey' in those days was the term for what is now 'Par' which didn't come into general use until the early 20th century.

Fortrose and Rosemarkie will never be in the first division of historic links courses; it is short by modern standards with little room for changing this. It has, however, hosted a number of amateur events such as the Scottish Ladies Seniors Open and the Scottish Club Championships as well as junior events. I do feel that it has a few weak holes but it remains a very classic test of links golf in a very attractive setting and that for me is why I will always want to return.

To find Glen Ord distillery, you return to the A9 and take the next junction north towards Muir of Ord, a small, attractive town in a low-lying agricultural area near the head of the Beauly Firth. Diageo is by some distance the market leader in

Scotch whisky and its Johnnie Walker brand is by far the largest Scotch whisky brand in the world, the only Scotch in the Top 10 of world whisky brands and over twice the size of the next Scotch. However, none of the top four Single Malt brands is owned by Diageo and their biggest brand, The Singleton, is an unusual one as it is actually an umbrella brand for three Single Malts. This requires some explanation. Single Malt Scotch whisky has to be matured and bottled in Scotland and has to be the product of one distillery. This regulation was brought in as some brands were using the term 'pure malt' for vatted products from more than one distillery. Also, some malts were from a single distillery but the brand and the distillery had become disconnected; that is, a well-known brand of malt was kept but its distillery had been closed and the production transferred elsewhere. The regulations state that there should be no use of a distillery name unless the product is made from that distillery. But there are exceptions (or rather exemptions): brands from long-closed distilleries can continue to make Single Malts as long as the name of the distillery in which it is produced is named on the front of the label. Stronachie is a good example; the Stronachie distillery was closed in the 1920s but the brand remains and is distilled at Benrinnes.

The Singleton is actually quite a new brand, launched in 2006, from three old distilleries: Glendullan dating from 1896, Dufftown from 1895 and, the oldest of them all, Glen Ord which dates back to 1838. Diageo clearly recognised their relative weakness in Single Malts (It is easier and more efficient to market fewer big brands than lots of small ones.) and this was a neat solution. Today, you have The Singleton, Dufftown, The Singleton, Glendullan and The Singleton, Glen Ord, each sub-brand able to have its own distinct characteristics and launch its own particular expressions under the single umbrella of The Singleton brand. There is also a geographical sales focus for each with the product tailored to that particular market: Glendullan for the US market, Dufftown for the European market and Glen Ord for the Asian market.

The American oak washbacks at the Glen Ord Distillery

The Glen Ord Distillery was founded by a Black Isle barley farmer, Thomas Mackenzie in 1838. It had various owners throughout the next one hundred years before being bought by Scottish Malt Distillers Ltd in 1930 and United Distillers, the forerunner of Diageo, in 1985. Diageo has steadily invested in increased capacity and today it is Diageo's second largest malt distillery. There are plans currently to increase this further while they are also investing in upgrading the visitor centre situated in the old distillery building. Just as Diageo with The Singleton looked to play catch-up in the Single Malt market, this is to some extent also true in the 'visitor centre' experience. The likes of The Glenlivet and Glenfiddich, the two biggest Single Malt Scotch brands, were for many years ahead of the Diageo sites in providing professional visitor experiences. As we will see in Chapter 8, Diageo is now investing in this across many of their sites as well as having a home in Edinburgh for its world-leading blended brand, Johnnie Walker. I visited Glen Ord before they had opened their new visitor centre but it is likely to be designed to be on a par with the substantial facilities which have been in existence for a while at Glenmorangie, The Glenlivet and Glenfiddich. Interestingly, The Macallan, after its substantial investment in an architecturally innovative new distillery, still only opens to visitors at weekends – it is very much a premium experience clearly targeted at brand devotees.

While the location is attractive the immediate entrance to the distillery is not attractive because the first building you see is a large maltings on a rather ugly, industrial-looking, site. Glen Ord is one of only two distilleries which does all its own malting and Glen Ord also produces malt for other Diageo sites such as Talisker on Skye. The old distillery comprises attractive Victorian stone buildings most of which will now be used as the new visitor centre as the increased capacity is being housed in newer and refurbished buildings behind. Inside, all is what you would expect from a traditional large malt distillery: mash tuns, American oak washbacks and fairly conventionally-shaped pot stills, neither as tall as Glenmorangie nor as squat as Macallan or even Glenfiddich.

The Singleton brand – 'Singleton' refers, I gather, to the last remaining cask in the warehouse – is clearly mass-targeted, and while each distillery version is tailored to its particular market, it is often regarded as an entry level malt so without any particularly distinctive characteristics. The Glen Ord version is not widely available in the UK and many whisky devotees were upset when in 2006 the original Glen Ord 12-year-old was discontinued as they saw it as a classic example of a smoother-style Highland malt. The distillery still releases occasional special editions for Diageo's Rare Malts series.

I'm probably giving the impression that there is nothing particularly distinctive about Glen Ord, be it the location, the distillery, the visitor experience nor, indeed, the product itself. This is perhaps true but it is an important part of this extraordinarily successful Scottish industry. This is a site that exports practically 100% of its product and is truly international in its focus. This was reflected on my tour; there were eleven of us, six Spaniards, two Americans, two Canadians and me. Indeed, that spring when I visited many distilleries, UK citizens were very much in the minority reflecting the global success of the industry. As such, while Glen Ord may not be the most exciting distillery visit you will make, it is emblematic of the industry and its international appeal and in that respect a good place to have started this latest tour.

**The delightful short Par 3 12th hole at Hopeman
with the gorse in full bloom**

**The wall behind the 8th green at Hopeman draws
comparisons with the 13th at North Berwick**

CHAPTER TWO

MORAYSHIRE

'With a fine sea view, and a clear course in front of him, the golfer should find no difficulty in dismissing all worries from his mind, and regarding golf, even if it may be indifferent golf, as the true and adequate end of man's existence.'

A J Balfour 1848-1930

U.K. Prime Minister and keen golfer

MORAY WAS THE destination of my third chapter in *Of Peats and Putts* and I make no apology for returning. This time I am using the ancient county name, Morayshire, as I intend to move on in the next chapter to Banffshire -both disappeared in the local government reorganisation of 1975 when Moray became a district of the Grampian region which included the Speyside whisky towns of Aberlour and Dufftown which originally had been in Banffshire.

While Speyside is Scotland's whisky heartland surprisingly few of its distilleries used to be open to the public. Until recently it could boast around half of all Scotland's producing distilleries but the huge number of new start-ups across the country has changed this. They were well-established whisky producers where the business model did not require a visitor centre. As the popularity of Single Malts has taken off and the whisky and tourism markets have come together, this has changed; start-ups have made visitor centres a core part of their business and their marketing and in some ways the big established brands have followed. I featured The Glenlivet (owned by Pernod Ricard) in *Of Peats and Putts* and you can now visit the likes of Macallan owned by Edrington and Glendronach owned by Brown Forman or go for a Chivas Regal Cellar tasting at Strathisla. All these are owned by big multinationals, like Diageo at Glen Ord. I also featured Benromach, a distillery which Gordon and McPhail had reopened in 1998. It is interesting to see that company, traditionally an independent bottler, further diversifying into distilling as they are now building from scratch a new distillery at Craggan, just west of Grantown-on-Spey. It is in a pretty spot, just off the A95 and very well placed for whisky tourism.

There is new investment everywhere. The new Macallan distillery near Craigellachie is an architect-designed, £140 million, innovative building, housing both the distillery and a visitor centre and, with its mound-shaped grassy roof, intended to sit sympathetically in its landscape. The roof has 1,800 single beams and 380,000 individual components and is visually arresting. Surprisingly, the visitor centre which includes an up-market bistro is routinely only open at weekends though this is extended to some Thursdays and Fridays in the summer. You can't really pop in for a £10 tour – instead you are offered various 'experiences' which start at £50 and include everything from picnic lunches and fishing on the estate to a chauffeured ride in a Bentley. Again, we see a famous name in whisky becoming a premium-brand 'experience'. While I don't for a moment suggest there is anything wrong with this, I am going to recommend something, just a couple of miles away, at the other end of the scale which nonetheless is probably more informative about the real world of whisky-making. For just £5 you can enjoy a 45-minute tour of the Speyside Cooperage and witness coopers applying their art in a critical part of the whisky-making process.

Speyside can offer some good golf from Spey Valley at Aviemore in the east to Spey Bay at the river's mouth on the coast. The former is a modern layout designed by Dave Thomas and part of a hotel resort while the latter dates back to 1907, designed by Ben Sayers with Prime Minister Ramsay MacDonald an early member. Recently it has been bought by an American 'crypto investment organisation' which raised the money from selling non-fungible tokens to its members. I'm not the one to explain how this works but it does demonstrate the wide appeal of Scotland's historic golfing assets. There is also, of course, the delightful Boat of Garten which I featured in my last book. This apart, my favourite courses are, however, those on the coast. Having featured the wonderful Moray club at Lossiemouth last time, I looked for other options. The two most highly rated courses are Castle Stuart and Nairn Golf Club while Nairn Dunbar, following some recent changes, has a growing reputation. Cullen is an attractive and fun links and there is an eccentric 9-hole links just along from Lossiemouth called Covesea. It's very pretty but actually a bit too eccentric even for me – two of the Par 3s are blind! A couple of miles further west is a real hidden gem: Hopeman, a delightful 'clifftop links' with wonderful views and a testing layout. Just as you can spend £400 on a full day's experience at Macallan to include fishing on the estate, you could also spend in excess of £200 to play at Castle Stuart or Nairn Golf Club. These are both magnificent courses with good clubhouses and worth a visit. However, as an alternative you could spend £30 for 18 holes on a twilight ticket and play on a challenging old clifftop links with stunning views over the Moray Firth and then enjoy refreshments in a friendly clubhouse afterwards. So, while Macallan and Castle Stuart would be the 'premium' experience for £600 plus, what I will feature – The Speyside Cooperage and Hopeman - will be, for under £50, the 'value' experience. What is important to remember is that 'value' doesn't mean inferior – in fact, I think in many ways you will learn more about the whisky industry and the history of golf from my chosen venues.

In the early part of the 19th century Hopeman had been a thriving herring fishing village. During the mid-century the shoals of herring disappeared and the village went into decline until the arrival of the railway started attracting tourists. A local laird offered up some land and a 9-hole course was founded in 1909. In 1922 an old wooden railway carriage became the first clubhouse and this distinctive feature survived until 1975 when a new one was built. The course was extended to 18 holes in 1985 and more recently the club has undergone further upgrades overseen by Mackenzie Ebert. Today it is a thriving club with a growing reputation.

The move to 18 holes is not immediately obvious except for holes 3-6 which lie on flattish land on the inland side of the clubhouse. The first two holes play away and back to the clubhouse respectively and are original ones. If holes 3-6 don't inspire, once you find yourself on the 7th tee there is plenty to admire on each hole. The Par 3 7th looks innocent which it is if you don't go long where you will find a burn surrounding the back of the green, something which wasn't apparent from the tee. 8 is an attractive short Par 4 narrowing to a green nestling beside a wall with echoes of North Berwick. This is a very pretty part of the course though the spectacular sea views are still to come. Holes 9, 10 and 11 are played along and back the cliff top on dramatically undulating fairways giving an extra premium to control especially with gorse and broom ever-present. Every shot requires thought rather than just strength. This brings us to the 12th tee which is a perfect spot to enjoy the views over the Moray Firth where on a clear day you can see the peak of Morvern, the highest point in Caithness. What you can also see is the famous Par 3 12th, the hole which Hopeman is best known for. It's called the Preishach which apparently means 'a dip in the land full of shrubs'. That is not a bad description. It's quite a short hole, less than 150 yards depending on the tee, but it plunges down 100 feet into Clashach Cove below surrounded by gorse on three sides and the beach on the other. There are two bunkers, one short left and the other mid-green right. Obviously, club selection is all-important and heavily dependent on the wind. It has been called 'the best Par 3 in the world'. It's funny, I have played quite a number of the 'best Par 3s in the world'! I played one at Cruet Island in Donegal only last year. It was Paul Lawrie, Scotland's Open Champion at Carnoustie in 1999, who called it the best Par 3 he had ever played and he is now the Club's Honorary President, a position once held by none other than Ramsay MacDonald, a native of nearby Lossiemouth. The hole is certainly a great one and very memorable. I was playing Hopeman by myself and hit my first shot straight at the pin but ended on the front of the green. It was a pretty good shot but I felt I could do better. I had a second go hitting the ball a little harder and a little further to the left, just over the left side bunker. This worked well as there is a slope on that side of the green which brought my ball back to the middle where the flag was. A 4-foot put gave me my birdie, albeit with my second ball. Awarding yourself a Mulligan is one of the pleasures of playing golf alone.

It's quite a steep walk back up the hill to the 13th tee though not so bad when you have hit the green and only need to take down your putter and not as tiring when you have made birdie. 13 and 14 again require accuracy as they are gorse-framed while the next short hole, 15, plays directly down and out to sea. It is another short Par 3 but there is no good place to miss. The toughest three holes on the course are the final three. 16 is quite a long dogleg Par 4 playing up the hill and bending right. Both the drive and the second need to be accurate and favouring the left. 17, in contrast to the previous Par 3s, is a monster. 220 yards uphill and when I played, into a wind. I was happy with 4. Equally the 18th is extremely tough, being the longest Par 4 on the course. While only around 400 yards it was again into the wind when I played, but the problem is the burn which runs across the fairway just short of the attractively positioned green which sits invitingly just in front of the clubhouse. When I played there was no option but to play the hole as a five; even two of my best would have risked going into the burn. Even then the final pitch over the burn is a shot which requires nerve; I can imagine there have been a few disasters at this hole in Club Medals over the years.

The course was well kept when I played and in good condition for April, the turf being very natural. An engaging feature are the local sandstone tee markers which come from the nearby Clashach quarry. This stone has a worldwide reputation and has been used in both the British Memorial Garden at Ground Zero in New York and the Sagrada Familia in Barcelona. Little features like this make a big difference. I recently played at quite a prestigious course which had plastic tee markers which I found a bit tacky and disappointing – a little effort and only a little more cost can make a big impression.

Hopeman, rather like Fortrose and Rosemarkie, is definitely the model for the types of courses and clubs I will increasingly want to visit. Playing Troon and Turnberry and Carnoustie may be top of many golfer's ambitions and I am fortunate to have played all of these. But rather than return all the time to these major venues, I think playing the likes of Hopeman brings just as much enjoyment and satisfaction. Frankly, for a mid-handicapper like me, they are a more realistic test while there is also the matter of cost. The Open venues are now charging upwards of £250 per round. I played Hopeman on a twilight ticket (twilight starting at a very civilised 3pm) for £30. The environment and views are as good as anywhere (certainly better than the likes of Carnoustie) and the welcome in the clubhouse inviting. Hopeman is a vibrant local club which is happy to welcome visitors. It's in a beautiful location. It's a good test of golf. What is not to like? If golf is about experiencing that 'joy to be alive' feeling, Hopeman on a sunny spring evening certainly delivered.

The heart of Speyside is probably a triangle of small towns, less than 10 miles apart: Rothes, Aberlour and Dufftown.

Rothes is the home of Glen Grant, now owned by Campari and the site of the now closed Caperdonich Distillery. Those who read my book on Europe may remember that its stills were purchased by The Owl Distillery in Belgium. Its site is now used by the well-known still makers, Forsyths, a business that had needed to expand its premises as it benefited from the boom in distillery start-ups. Forsyths has even purchased the Station Hotel in Rothes which has been handsomely refurbished, no doubt helping them entertain their many customers from around Scotland and overseas. We will be heading to Dufftown in the next chapter but on the way, in the centre of this triangle, sits another small town, Craigellachie, where The Speyside Cooperage was founded by the Taylor family in 1947. In 1991 it moved to a new site just outside the small town on the road towards Dufftown. Like many whisky distilleries, it is now owned by a multinational company and again it is the French who invested, with Tonnellerie Francois Frères Group purchasing the business in 2008. TFF Group's origins are unsurprisingly in wine cooperage but also encompass forestry, cask and stainless-steel vat making. The whisky and bourbon cooperage business comprises seven sites, four in Scotland and three in the US. Again, we see two themes: the global nature of the industry and the strong presence of French businesses.

You may have been impressed if you have visited the Great Pyramids of Giza but the great pyramids of whisky barrels at Speyside Cooperage are no less dramatic and can be seen from some distance. The site is quite a sprawling one and is a hive of activity. The tour starts with a short video and then consists of witnessing this activity from a mezzanine viewing-gallery above the main production area.

I don't need to reprise in any detail the important role of quality casks in the production of malt whisky and the symbiotic relationship between the US bourbon industry, which requires that fresh casks can only be used once, and the Scotch industry, that relies on used bourbon barrels of American white oak (quercus alba) as its main maturing

The entrance to the fascinating Speyside Cooperage

medium. For Scotch Whisky, all maturing has to be done in oak which it has been known for centuries has the best properties for maturation with its tight grain being leak resistant yet allowing the liquid to breathe while slowly releasing tannins which impart colour and flavour. First-fill bourbon barrels used to be broken down to be transported from America but nowadays they are generally shipped intact, so today the cooper's role is more about maintenance and refurbishment. The Speyside Cooperage undertakes a number of processes depending on its customers' requirements but essentially its core service is repairing and reconditioning barrels on behalf of distilleries. Most large distilleries or distillery groups will have their own purchase arrangements for barrels but may need those barrels to be repaired or reconditioned in some way: toasted, de-charred, re-charred or charcoaled depending on the age and source of the barrel and the particular style the distillery is seeking.

The production floor has both trained coopers and apprentices distinguished by whether they are wearing blue or red. Apprenticeships generally take four years and once they have been completed, trained coopers get the honour of being 'tarred and feathered' in a barrel. Apparently, this ancient ritual called 'trussing the cooper' dates from the 14th century and used to involve actual tar and feathers but today health and safety policies dictate that this particular rite of passage simply involves being covered in some gunge and rolled about in a barrel. It is reckoned that there are now about 300 coopers in Scotland with apprenticeship opportunities over-subscribed. While all the coopers I saw were male, Diageo announced in 2019 that they had taken on their first ever female apprentices. The Speyside Cooperage is increasing its workforce significantly through an apprentice scheme to meet the market growth.

'Disciplined freneticism' is probably the best way of describing the activity on show in the production area, where the coopers scamper about working on various different processes using a variety of tools and machines. Some of these have colourful names: a croze board and an adze, a borer, a bick iron and a belly knife, a scullup, a shiv and a swarth. Don't ask what each of these are but they demonstrate that coopers do a wide range of tasks, from making a new barrel from a plank of wood to repairing and reconditioning old ones in various different ways. Essentially making a barrel requires connecting wooden staves with hoops and adding a top and a bottom (called 'heads' or 'headers'). These are craft skills with limited automation and the quality and efficiency is determined by the skill and expertise of the employees rather than anything else. That they are apparently paid by the barrel which perhaps accounts for the impressive pace of work. In recent years they held a competition to determine if their coopers could make a 190-litre barrel in under 7 minutes 30 seconds. The winner did it in less than half that time, an incredible 3 minutes 3 seconds, and now has his name in the Guinness Book of Records. But above all it is the skill which impresses, so having an apprentice scheme is critical to the company's sustainability, ensuring that these skills do not die out.

The visitor centre has a pleasant café and shop but is in many ways quite down-to-earth. And that is what I liked about this visit – it is not really a 'visitor centre' but a production site which welcomes visitors. It is not heavily marketed but simply demonstrates exactly how the process operates. There are no shiny stills or architect-designed distillery buildings with pagoda roofs to take pictures of. The building is of a standard factory type – it is unpretentious because it is the real thing. I would encourage anyone who has been on many distillery tours to add a visit to the Speyside Cooperage as it will give an added dimension to their understanding of the product and the industry. In a similar way, I would encourage those who come to play Castle Stuart and Nairn also to make time for the likes of Hopeman where they will get a surprisingly rewarding experience for a fraction of the price.

The impressive new still house at Glenfiddich

The backdrop of the famous seven arch Banff Bridge over the
Deveron dominates the challenging 17th hole at Duff House Royal.
The original bridge dates from 1779 and was widened in 1881.

CHAPTER THREE

BANFFSHIRE

'Aye, but today's rain is tomorrow's whisky.'

Ancient Scottish proverb

USING THE ANCIENT county of Banffshire has enabled me to play a clever trick and feature another Speyside classic because the town of Dufftown, while less than five miles from the Speyside Cooperage at Craigellachie in old Morayshire, is situated across the ancient county border. Dufftown is home to many famous Scotch whisky names: Mortlach, The Balvenie and of course Glenfiddich, owned by William Grant & Sons, now a multinational spirits business but still family owned and deserving a central role in any book on the Scotch whisky industry.

For the golf in this chapter, we are headed towards the coast but it is the first of three inland courses in this book: Duff House Royal, in the historic county town of Banff. For a links enthusiast there has to be good reason to include it and that is a combination of its delightful setting and the history of the club and the course, one designed by no less than Alister MacKenzie. The town is attractive, dating back to the 10th century but today is dominated by lots of classic

Georgian and Victorian buildings. Banff is said to have more listed buildings than any other town in Scotland. There is also a link between Dufftown and Banff; the clock on the handsome pink granite tower that dominates Dufftown is known as 'the clock that hanged Macpherson' and originated in Banff. There in 1701, a local vagabond named James Macpherson had been sentenced to death by the gallows but was expecting a reprieve following a petition from some locals. Cannily the local sheriff circumvented this by moving the clock an hour forward so that the petition didn't arrive in time.

Let's start in Dufftown which is an attractive small town and the Glenfiddich distillery with its Victorian buildings set amongst smartly landscaped gardens alongside a burn (a Scottish word for a stream) and a lochan (a Scottish word for a pond). I visited in spring and the masses of daffodils completed a delightful setting. As well as ducks enjoying the environment of the distillery, I was surprised to see a couple of oystercatchers which the tour guide said were regular visitors. I gather from some of my bird-watching friends that it is not unusual for oystercatchers to stray from their more familiar coastal habitats, especially by following a river upstream. While the setting is quiet and fairly rural, this is not some small, quaint whisky distillery; this is Scotland's largest malt distillery (perhaps now equal with The Glenlivet) with the capacity to produce 21 million litres of pure alcohol annually. What is impressive is that this has been achieved here at the original distillery location and the latest investment in particular has been sympathetically integrated into the site.

The reception area proudly displays pictures of the family tree which leads from William Grant and his wife Elizabeth

Grant who founded the business in 1887 to the family members who are still involved in the business today of which there are at least six. Perhaps the two most influential figures in the history after the founders are the great grandsons Charles Grant Gordon and Alexander Grant Gordon. These two brothers took over the business in the early 1950s on the premature death of their father, with Charles focusing on investing in a large grain distillery in Girvan for their famous *Grants Stand Fast* blended brand (*Stand Fast* being the family motto) and Sandy (Alexander) launching the malt used in this blend as a 'Straight Malt'. While some 'straight malt' (i.e. not blended) had been sold since the early part of the 20th century the vast majority of malt was produced for the big brands of blends which had powered the Scotch whisky market from late Victorian times. In this respect it was Glenfiddich (Glenfiddich means 'valley of the deer') which invented the 'Single Malt' market which today is driving market growth. The other big players soon noticed the success of Glenfiddich during the 1960s and followed, especially Glenmorangie and The Glenlivet. Today global marketing of Scotch Malt Whisky is an established business but it was Grants which started this in the early 1960s, marketing the Glenfiddich brand in the same distinctive triangular bottle which had been used for the Grants blend.

The success of the 'straight malt' or 'pure malt' market led to various updates of the legal definition of whisky with the Scotch Whisky Regulations of 2009 clarifying nomenclature and banning descriptions like 'pure malt', 'straight malt' and 'vatted malt'. There are now five categories: Single Malt (a product of just one distillery), Single Grain, Blended Whisky,

Blended Malt and Blended Grain – I use capital letters for these to reflect that they are legal definitions.

Today Glenfiddich remains the world's biggest selling Single Malt brand though every year it has a close tussle with The Glenlivet for that distinction. But William Grant has been an innovator in other areas. In its whisky portfolio it also markets The Balvenie (like The Glenlivet, the definitive article is part of the brand) from the distillery next door and The Balvenie brand was one of the first to market a sherry finishing malt in the early 1980s – it is now known as The Balvenie Doublewood. It now also markets the successful Blended Malt (a malt from more than one distillery), Monkey Shoulder, recognised as one of the leading brands in this sector. Monkey Shoulder, named after a muscular repetitive strain condition suffered by maltsters while turning over the drying malt with a large shovel, is a blend of malts from William Grant's three Dufftown distilleries – Glenfiddich, Balvenie and Kininvie – and is a smooth, malty blend which works well with ice or in a cocktail. Then in 2010 it recognised the growth potential of Irish Whiskey and bought the Tullamore D.E.W. brand and immediately set about building a new distillery in County Offaly – the original one had closed down in 1954. Finally, they have expanded into other spirits with the successful Hendricks Gin created in 1999 as well as brands of rum and tequila and the acquisition of Drambuie in 2014. More recent innovations include the 'Discarded' brand producing spirits such as rum, vodka and vermouth from process waste material and Atopia a brand of non-alcoholic spirit, a market which by all accounts is showing significant growth. All these brands can now be bought through the company's own consumer-facing ecommerce website called 'Clink'. It is hugely encouraging to see a family-owned Scottish business successfully investing and innovating and becoming a global leader in its field.

No 12 of the extraordinary 48 Douglas fir washbacks at Glenfiddich

As you would expect, the visitor centre, tour and shop are all professionally organised. You get an idea of the scale of the operation; there are now forty-eight douglas fir washbacks and an extraordinary forty-three stills – sixteen wash stills and twenty-seven spirit stills. If the old still house is impressive, the new one is even more so. Having double the amount of spirit stills to wash stills is their distinctive approach to distilling. The stills are quite small so the output of each wash still run is split between two spirit stills, which are a different shape to the wash stills, to increase the copper contact.

The other distinctive approach worth mentioning is the use of their 'Solera vat' in maturing their 15-year-old spirit. Inspired by the sherry bodegas of Spain, this huge vat is used to blend nearly matured casks before the contents are put into marrying tuns. The vat is never emptied so some of the whisky will be very old as it was first set up in 1998. It is claimed that not only does it produce a more complex product but that the process enables a more consistent one. The other point to make is that with the scale of the business and the focus on aged malts, they require forty-seven warehouses to house their maturing spirit.

I would also commend the tasting after the tour. Most tours include a tasting of perhaps a couple of the distillery's products. At Glenfiddich you are taken inside to a smart tasting room and given drams of four of their core products; the 12-year-old, the 15-year-old, an 18-year-old and a 21-year-old. The tasting is facilitated and each product explained; the core 12 being 85% bourbon, 15% sherry; the 15-year-old, using the solera vat is 70% bourbon, 20% sherry and 10% from fresh oak barrels; the 18-year-old is 80% bourbon and 20% sherry and the 21-year-old, 95% bourbon, 5% sherry and then finished for four months in a rum cask. Having this explained as you taste each is perfect for both the whisky expert and, like me, the amateur enthusiast. Distilleries could do more to pay a little more attention to the detail of how they offer their tastings. For drivers a 'nosing kit' and drivers' drams are available – this has now, rightly, become common practice.

It is about a 45-minute drive to Banff through the mainly agricultural Aberdeenshire countryside. There are nearer distilleries to Banff which I could have featured. Glenglassaugh, situated near the coast between Cullen and Portsoy, has three times closed and been reopened since it was founded in 1873. Its most recent reopening in 2008 was also not an immediate success and the distillery was bought in 2013 by the BenRiach Distillery Company founded by the well-known industry figure, Billy Walker. However, it was probably the poor relation to BenRiach and GlenDronach, the other two distillery brands in that portfolio, and didn't receive much investment. BenRiach was then bought in 2016 by Brown Forman, the American multinational owner of Jack Daniels, who were also investors in the new Slane distillery in Ireland. Glenglassaugh is therefore a relatively unknown brand and while it is yet to be seen how significantly Brown Forman will invest in it, having a cash-rich multinational owner is probably a good thing.

Banff itself has a long history in distilling. The main Banff distillery had a chequered history of ownership and eventually closed in 1983 in the 'whisky recession' of that era. The distillery had had an unfortunate history of fires. The first occurred in 1877 completely destroying the main buildings but these were immediately rebuilt and the business prospered for a while before closing during the 1930s. While it was not producing, the site held plenty stock and in 1941 a warehouse was struck by a German bomber causing the maturing barrels of whisky to explode dramatically. Allegedly, with the whisky escaping into the local burn and watercourses, nearby grazing cows and wildlife became intoxicated! Production re-started after the war and a further explosion occurred in 1959 causing significant damage and then after its closure in 1983 yet another fire in 1991 during demolition finally brought to an end its rather incendiary history. However, distilling still takes place in the town on the other side of the riverbank from the golf course where the Macduff distillery was founded in 1958 by a Scottish consortium. Today, the distillery is part of Bacardi's John Dewar & Sons portfolio and, as well as producing malt for the successful William Lawson's export blend, it now produces a single malt called The Deveron after the river on which it sits.

The River Deveron also dominates the golf course which we will visit: Duff House Royal. The Deveron can be regarded as a 'hidden gem' of Scottish rivers, not as famous as its neighbour the Spey but still with a great reputation for its Atlantic salmon and sea and brown trout fishing. Duff House Royal which sits on the western bank just before the mouth of the river, is the only golf club in the world to have a Royal suffix rather than prefix and this allows me to explain its history. Alexander, 6th Earl of Fife and owner of Duff House, was the founder patron of the club, gifting the house and surrounding land to the local community in 1906 which led to the club being formed and the course opening in 1920. In 1889 he had married Princess Louise, the eldest daughter of the Prince of Wales. Princess Louise, known as the Princess Royal after the death of her husband, asked to become Patroness of the club and bestowed on it the Royal suffix as it appeared in her own title. She also conferred Royal status on the nearby Royal Tarlair Golf Club in the neighbouring town of Macduff. Royal Tarlair is worth playing for its sea views, rather different from the gentler river views at Duff House and, not unlike Hopeman, as a course is best remembered for a very dramatic Par 3 on the back nine.

You can still visit Duff House, now managed by Historic Scotland, a superb example of an 18th-century country house designed by William Adam. The library contains more than

4,000 books, there are furniture and china collections as well as many fine paintings from the National Galleries of Scotland, including examples of El Greco, Gainsborough, Raeburn, Ramsay and Etty.

The first layout in 1910 was designed by Archie Simpson of Royal Aberdeen fame and was opened with a match between J H Taylor and James Braid in that year. Today's layout, however, was the work of MacKenzie in 1924, just after the club had been given its Royal status.

Duff House Royal delivers top-class parkland golf in a delightful setting. This is not a course to inspire wonder or excitement and at under 6,100 yards off the white tees it doesn't feel that long but the Par of 68 is very challenging. While the land is fairly flat and there are no significant elevation changes, the greens are often slightly raised with tricky undulations and it was immaculately presented when I played there in late April. Also, it rather lulls you into a false sense of satisfaction with your play as the back 9 is very much harder than the front 9 as I experienced. I played the front 9 pretty much to my handicap which is always satisfying when playing a course for the first time – I could bore you by talking you through my birdie 2 on the 6th. But I hadn't studied the card. The front 9 has only one Par 4 over 400 yards; the back 9 has four. And when I played the wind was a cold one coming from the north-east off the Moray Firth and the back 9 played mainly into it. Life got considerably tougher. Five relatively benign Par 4s to start are all gently shaped before you arrive at the short 6th (did I mention I got a birdie there?) from where you head up along the river to another good Par 3 at 9 with a green set at an awkward angle beside the river. This is the furthest point of the course from the clubhouse and is where the real challenge of Duff House Royal starts. The next 8 holes bring you four Par 4s over 400 yards (two of which are over 450 yards), the course's only Par 5 and three par 3s which are, respectively, 205 yards, 176 yards (unfortunately into a strong wind when I played) and 237 yards. Yes, a 237 yards Par 3 and it's not downhill but was also straight into a three-club wind the day I played. Even if the wind had been behind, it would have been a challenge. To reach would require you to open your shoulders for a big hit and is that sensible with the River Deveron hugging the edge of the fairway? I was happy to get there in two by playing cautiously short and left. 16 (this long Par 3) and 17 (455 yards Par 4), both with the river sitting in a rather intimidating fashion on your right, are certainly the toughest holes on the course and it was something of a relief to head back to the clubhouse on 18, a relatively short Par 4 with a pleasant green sitting up in front of the clubhouse.

For what is essentially a flattish, parkland setting, this is a great course and definitely worthy of its place in most Top 100 surveys of courses in Scotland. The hole designs are thoughtful, the greens and surrounds are well shaped – in this respect in particular it bears the hallmark of a MacKenzie course - and it is all well-kept. The park has many lovely trees, you get glimpses of the imposing Duff House on the back 9, the River Deveron is pretty and the seven arch Banff bridge presents a dramatic background to the long 17th hole. And while it is in no way a links experience it is almost on the coast and so wind will frequently be a very significant factor.

The club also had a pleasant vibe to it. When visiting a new club, I often wonder whether I would like to be a member at it.

Duff House Royal would certainly do for me. I had organised to play with a friend in their Senior Open – these events are very common at Scottish clubs. The club was busy not only with visitors for the Open but, in the afternoon, members were pouring in to play. There were lots of lady golfers and youngsters. This was a club that clearly was supported by all the community. The welcome in the clubhouse was friendly and the atmosphere relaxed. Perhaps the only slightly intimidating aspect was the first tee which sits only a few feet from the front of the clubhouse; you almost feel that your backswing might hit it but it is actually a nice feature.

A quick word about Open events. These seem to be much more prevalent at Scottish clubs than in England. They come in many formats; straight Opens, Senior Opens, Pairs and Mixed Pairs events. Whatever the format, they invite players with handicaps from other clubs to come and play in their event at a very reasonable price – normally akin to the members' visitor green fee rather than the normal visitor green fee. The club gets a full day of green fees plus strong bar and catering takings and good PR about their course and visitors get to play a competitive round at a different course for tremendous value. Everybody wins. It's also, as ever with golf, an opportunity to meet other people. I had signed up with a friend to play but we played in a three ball with member from Forres which added greatly to the enjoyment of the day.

The view from the 9th tee at Cruden Bay is one of the best in golf.
The ruins of Slains Castle can just be seen in the distance

The meandering burn across the Par 5 13th hole at Cruden Bay

ABERDEENSHIRE

'The charm of the seaside courses of Great Britain lies in their multiformity, their unconventionality, their infinite variety.'

Robert Hunter (1874-1942)
The Links

BANFF IS ACTUALLY now in the modern-day administrative county of Aberdeenshire but I am going to head east towards the North Sea coast. Given the size of Aberdeenshire, it is surprising perhaps that I excluded it from my first book especially since it can offer a rich source of golfing options, particularly on the coast. The truth is that, despite its size, it has never been a major area for distilling, even though its agricultural heritage makes it an important area for growing barley. Mention should be made of Glendronach at Forgue near Huntly on the eastern fringes of the county. As I noted in the last chapter, this is now part of the Brown Forman portfolio but it has a distinguished history, incorporating many famous names in the Scotch whisky industry. It was built in 1826 by James Allardice along with a small group of entrepreneurial farming colleagues who saw the opportunity for the revival of legal distilling afforded by the 1823 Excise Act. Later, new

investment was forthcoming from a Walter Scott (not the one you are thinking of) and the expanded distillery became one of the biggest in the Highlands during the second half of the century. Following the Great War, it was bought by Charles Grant, son of the founder of Glenfiddich, then in 1960 by Teachers which expanded production using it as a source of malt for its famous Highland Cream blend. Teachers was bought by Allied Breweries, subsequently Allied Distillers, which was taken over by the French multi-national Pernod Ricard in 2005. The distillery had been mothballed between 1996 and 2002 and it soon came clear that Pernod Ricard wanted to focus on its The Glenlivet and Chivas Regal brands and didn't require the capacity. This was when it was bought by BenRiach which subsequently sold to Brown Forman. In 2022 Brown Forman announced a £30 million investment to double capacity at the site.

The coastal region of Aberdeenshire has only a modest history of distilling, the only other distillery of note being Glenugie near Peterhead. It enjoyed a colourful ownership history including an American conglomerate and, for a short time, Hugh Fraser (Lord Fraser of Allander, of House of Fraser fame) before ending up with the brewing group Whitbread which closed the distillery during the industry downturn of the 1980s.

As I plan to visit the most southerly mainland distillery at Bladnoch, the most easterly, NcNean, and the most northerly, the new 8 Stills at John O'Groats in my third book, it would make sense to feature the most easterly which nowadays is actually Brewdog at Ellon. This was opened as the Lone Wolf distillery in 2017 but has now been renamed Brewdog to take advantage of the strong brand awareness which this successful new brewer has developed. From my perspective however, I think this is very much a brewery with distilling attached rather than a focused distillery and so I am going to visit what has been accepted for many years as the most easterly: Glen Garioch at Oldmeldrum.

The traditional pagoda roof at the Glen Garioch Distillery in Oldmeldrum

I mentioned the east Aberdeenshire coast as being a rich source of golfing greatness. Putting aside the new Trump International course, which by all accounts is a magnificent design (not a surprise as it was a Martin Hawtree creation), the fifty-mile stretch of coastline from Fraserburgh in the farthest north corner down to Aberdeen offers plenty of gems. Fraserburgh, the seventh oldest, and Peterhead, the eighteenth oldest, are both worth playing and have at least eighteen excellent holes between them as well as offering fine views. Both, Peterhead in particular, have rather disappointing starts but they are worth a visit. In Aberdeen you have Royal Aberdeen and neighbouring Murcar which are two of my favourite courses in all of Scotland – I have often called the front 9 at Royal Aberdeen one of the most exhilarating stretch of holes in links golf. Murcar too is an exciting course with again the front 9 providing one memorable hole after another. Don't miss out either on Newburgh on Ythan. This 18-hole course is in fact one old 9 of traditional links and a new 9 built on higher land behind an impressively designed new clubhouse. If the new 9 offers some fun holes with wonderful views, the old 9 delivers proper, traditional links golf with all its subtleties in the peaceful surroundings of the Ythan estuary. Understated perhaps but none the worse for it. And if your golf is not at its best, you can just admire the Forvie National Nature Reserve with its dunes and mudflats which provide a regular refuelling stop for many migrating seabirds. But my choice is another great golfing location, Cruden Bay, almost exactly halfway between Aberdeen and Peterhead where as well as the world-renowned main course there is an underrated 9-hole layout, the St Olaf, which you should not miss out on.

Cruden Bay was one of a number of courses commissioned by The Great North Railway Company along with a grand luxury hotel to attract holiday makers. It was designed by Old Tom Morris and Archie Simpson and opened in 1899 with a two-day tournament including many famous names from Archie Simpson himself to James Braid, Ben Sayers and Harry Vardon, the eventual winner. The course was, however, significantly redeveloped in 1926 by Tom Simpson and Herbert Fowler and it is broadly their layout which we play today. They also at this time laid out the 9-hole St Olaf course. The old pink granite hotel sadly fell into disrepair and was demolished in the early 1950s when it was replaced by a new clubhouse on the same site. Today's clubhouse dates from 1998 and while architecturally it is a rather bland edifice, it occupies an unrivalled position, high above the links offering one of the best views from a clubhouse in golf. You can see almost the whole course set out below as well as views along the coast with the rather ghostly ruins of Slains Castle to the north believed to be where Bram Stoker got his inspiration for Count Dracula's castle.

Cruden Bay rather stands out amongst the courses I am choosing in this book as it is one of the top-rated in Scotland – 11th in the list I am using at time of writing. Increasingly I am avoiding the 'big names' as I find them both very expensive and the experience at times rather intimidating. As they are a magnet for visitors, in particular those from overseas, they can be busy and the golf often slow. Sometimes you get the feeling that you are being told it is a privilege to play there and you just have to fit in. Nothing could be further from the truth with my recent visit to Cruden Bay in April 2022. I was playing with a local friend and rang to book a time. The green fee is reasonable for a course of this standing. Knowing that we were a 2 ball we were advised what time was best to play to avoid being behind fourball visiting groups. The greeting was genuine and not contrived. The green fee not only includes 9 holes on the St Olaf but as many practice balls on the range as you like and a bottle of 'birdie juice' which is none other than a miniature of Cruden Bay commissioned Malt Whisky! As you can tell, I was impressed.

Cruden Bay is an excellent example of Robert Hunter's observation about the charm of seaside courses because it is certainly neither uniform nor conventional. Hunter was an American social reformer and amateur golfer and his remarkable book, *The Links*, first published in 1926, is a bible for golf course architects. He was not a golf architect himself but expresses strong views on the rights and wrongs of good course design. He comes down firmly on the side of natural terrain being used to full effect and witnesses many of the great links courses of the Scotland and England. He also recognises the importance of having the right soil: 'The most desirable soil is a well-drained, sandy loam, porous enough to dry quickly after heavy rain. Pure sand is very desirable, but it is nearly always necessary to mix other soils with it'. Cruden Bay doesn't get a mention but he would certainly have been a fan, with the exception perhaps of the Par 3 15th ('Blind one-shot holes are most undesirable'). He also, like Alister MacKenzie, believed that design should not attempt to make the game 'fair' as that would reduce its fundamental appeal.

We were very lucky as it was a superb spring day; bright and sunny though with a fresh (Scottish for 'cold') breeze coming off the North Sea. The course was in excellent condition. I have said that the course is highly rated but it is interesting that on its website the ranking it seems most proud of is being voted 2nd in a list of the UK and Ireland's Top 100 'Fun courses to play' in 2012. This was second to North Berwick, which I can understand, though I notice in 2021 it slipped to third place behind the Old Course at St Andrews which I don't understand.

Playing St Andrews is obviously a wonderful experience and a lot of fun but Cruden Bay delivers many more 'fun' holes. Cruden Bay delivers fun and a serious test of golf at the same time.

The first hole is played from in front of the delightful starter's hut, which actually used to be the old clubhouse, and is a relatively benign introduction to the course; you need simply to keep it straight, but the fun soon starts and thereafter almost every hole delivers something memorable. There is the 2nd with its dramatically raised green; the short Par 4 3rd with its cannily hidden green nesting by the estuary; the magnificent Par 3 4th along the side of the estuary with the old fishing village of Port Errol on the other side; the towering tee shot at the long Par 4 5th; the Par 5, 6th with its tricky third shot over a burn into the green; the delightfully dune-framed second shot up to the 7th green and the deceptively difficult short Par 4, 8th, only 250 yards with no bunkers, yet where a four is never a given. The green is picturesquely situated surrounded by enormously high dunes. Time to draw breath, particularly as you now climb up the dune to the 9th tee from where you get one of the greatest views in golf with a 360-degree panorama and all the golf course in view.

I am sure that there are lots of other candidates for 'the greatest view in golf'. I'm drawn to seaside examples as they tend to be more dramatic and far-reaching and many of the great links offer them: from the clubhouse at Moray, the 1st tee at Machrihanish, the 5th tee at Sheringham, the 8th tee at St Enodoc, the 5th tee at Rosses Point, County Sligo, the 18th tee at Tralee, the 7th Tee at Ballyliffen and many on the Donegal courses. Perhaps for inland courses the 11th tee at Royal

Ashdown Forest is hard to beat. I could go on and I am sure that there are more, particularly in the United States but this will compete with the best of them.

The 9th is the main recent change made to the course by the design firm Mackenzie Ebert and they have done a great job. If I remember rightly, the old 9th was simply a rather featureless straight hole along the top of the dune which then takes you to the next part of the course. The new tee has been brought to a dramatic position on the edge of the dune and the hole is now a long slight dog-leg to a green which perches on the far edge of the dune. I say dune but it is more like walking on top of a cliff. I probably particularly approved of this new hole as I managed to hit a long second shot in to about 8 feet. The 10th tee has also been moved and you play dramatically downhill to the links below with the second shot needing to carry a burn. The 11th is a short Par 3 playing back the way over the burn again to a green at an awkward angle. 12 is perhaps a rest from the drama; it is, however, a very good links hole with some classic features, notably three nasty pot bunkers. 12 is a long Par 5 (if it is into the wind it will feel *very* long) and you need to concentrate as the burn meanders drunkenly across the fairway. Such is its meander, from the right-hand side of the fairway you have to cross it three times with your second shot so you need to make sure you have enough club. If you succeed in this you still have a difficult uphill shot to the green which, again, is slightly hidden behind a dune. Having played a number of Tom Simpson courses in Europe, his Par 5s are often noteworthy and this, as well as the 6th, the only other one on the course, is a great example. It is not a case of just belting three shots in the right direction; each shot gives you options and requires some care. 13 is stroke index 2 and can simply be described as 'narrow' so keep it straight. While the narrow fairway gathers from the sides, miss it at your peril as anything wide will be punished horribly. Again, the green is hidden, this time in a delightful sunken dell. The Par 3 15th takes hidden greens to an extreme. Yes, it's the famous blind Par 3. It's nearly 200 yards and so a good hit is required and you aim for a post on the side of the hill and hope for the best. The green is actually generously sized but much depends on the pin position. It's fun. There follows a much more conventional Par 3, a downhill shot to an attractively placed green.

If there is a weakness at Cruden Bay, it is probably 17 and 18, two Par 4s which take you back to the clubhouse. They are not bad holes, indeed they are perfectly good holes, but somehow lack the exhilaration of what you have just experienced and thereby suffer by comparison. But that is a rather unfair complaint as, from a golfing perspective, they both require concentration to complete a good score.

After an excellent fish and chips in the clubhouse we played the St Olaf in the afternoon. It is set on much flatter ground between the 1st and 18th holes on the old course and the main links. However, it is authentic links golf and a good post-prandial outing with four Par 3s, all of which test the accuracy of your strike.

Sometimes when you return to a course you haven't played for a long time, it can be a disappointment. Maybe you played well the first time or the weather was perfect and the return can be a slight let down. I am now wary of that but with Cruden Bay the whole experience from the greeting in both the Pro Shop and the Clubhouse, to the course and its condition, the food, not to mention the weather, was, if anything, ahead of my expectations. There are lessons for other clubs, I feel. Not every club is blessed with a course which can deliver such a combination of fun and excellence but any club can go that extra mile in greeting and looking after its visitors and making sure it provides good food and friendly service. I will return soon I hope.

Oldmeldrum is an attractive small town about half-an-hour inland from Cruden Bay, some five miles north of the bigger and better known market town of Inverurie. Agriculture is probably the main activity though both towns are within easy commuter reach of Aberdeen so have attracted workers in what was for a while a growing oil-service industry. The distillery is near the centre of the town on the northern side and is located in the original buildings with a public road dividing the site. Parking for visitors is quite restricted though you can easily walk from the town centre. There is a small, smart visitor centre and a shop with regular tours. It probably benefits from being the only old distillery within easy reach of Aberdeen.

Glen Garioch (pronounced *Glen Geery*) dates back to the 18th century and has also been through many different owners, as well as enduring two periods of being mothballed. It became part of the Distillers' Company in the 1930s when that company acquired Booth's distillers which had recently merged with Sanderson's, the owner since 1908. William Sanderson was a distinguished industry figure in late Victorian times, beginning as a wine and spirits dealer in Leith in the 1860s. He was one of those who saw the opportunity for blending grain and malt spirit following the passing of the 1860 Spirits Act. He created the famous VAT 69 brand which is still successful today and it was in looking for malt spirit for this blend that he became part-owner of Glen Garioch in 1886. He was also one of the founders of the huge North British grain distillery in Edinburgh and so was one of the pioneers of Scotch blended whisky which was the foundation of today's world-renowned industry.

Glen Garioch became a victim of Distillers' rationalisation programme in the early 1970s before being bought by Stanley Morrison who already owned Bowmore. Morrisons Bowmore was to become a notable success story of the industry in the following two decades, also acquiring Auchentoshan in 1984. A decade later the business was acquired by Suntory. Today this is Beam Suntory following Suntory's acquisition of Beam inc. thereby adding the Teachers, Ardmore and Laphroaig Scotch brands to the portfolio. Teachers, as noted earlier, had many years ago included malt distilled at GlenDronach. Sometimes, ownership and the interconnectedness of distilleries in Scotch whisky (as in many other industries) is quite complicated to follow. Indeed, Beam Suntory has a sales, marketing and distribution joint venture with the private Edrington Group which adds Macallan, Highland Park, Glenrothes and Famous Grouse brands to the stable.

Beam Suntory is actually the world's third largest producer of premium spirits after Diageo and Pernod Ricard. In addition to its Scotch portfolio, it sells Jim Beam, Maker's Mark, Canadian Club, Courvoisier, Sipsmith gin and the Japanese whisky brands, Yamazaki, Hakushu and Hibiki. And this spirits division is just a part of the even bigger Suntory which also sells soft drinks, beer, wine and health foods. So, Glen Garioch is just a very, very small part of an enormous global business yet it doesn't feel like that. The site has benefited from significant investment which is clearly the benefit of being part of a global business. What is interesting is the nature of that investment. Two of the upgrades are investments in 'old technology', namely the replacement of indirect heating of its wash still with directly gas-fired heating and the re-installation of floor maltings which had been removed in 1995 and which is now quite a rarity in Scottish distilleries, though two of the other remaining floor maltings are at Laphroaig and Bowmore, two Islay distilleries which are also part of the Beam Suntory portfolio. This suggests that despite being a Japanese-owned global business it is very much run by management steeped in the history of Scotch Whisky. Very often it is the new challenger businesses, the start-ups, which seek differentiation in process technology with a nod to tradition rather than efficiency. It is encouraging to see a large business doing just this.

All the production is now of single malts so, as you would expect, there are many new expressions being produced, from a core non-age statement 1797 Founders' Reserve to a 12-year-old. As well as other aged releases, recently a new range of cask bottlings has been released called the Glen Garioch Renaissance Collection. This is a multi-national company with global reach and many different markets to service and so will tailor different products to these varying market requirements. While Glen Garioch is owned by a huge global player it remains a relatively small distillery – that is the beauty of the malt whisky market. Production scale is not a central issue so small distinctive production sites will survive as multinational players need a portfolio of brands for a market which supports almost endless segmentation.

**The new Arbikie Distillery has a range of still types
to enable its broad range of distillations**

**Coastal erosion has necessitated the re-shaping
of the second hole at Montrose**

CHAPTER FIVE

ANGUS

'A good gulp of whisky at bedtime –
it's not very scientific but it helps.'

Alexander Fleming (1881-1955)
Scottish physician

DRIVING SOUTH FROM Aberdeen, the first ancient county you come to is what used to be Kincardineshire. I suggest that you come off the main A90 and visit Stonehaven, a pretty fishing port which also boasts a dramatic cliff-top golf course. Nearby you will find Ury Castle, the location for a proposed new 'golf village' comprising housing and a Jack Nicklaus designed golf course. The A90 route south to Dundee has recently been witnessed around the world as that taken by the cortege which drove the late Queen Elizabeth's coffin from Balmoral Castle on nearby Deeside to Edinburgh, the first stage of its journey to her final resting place in Windsor Castle. However, I would again recommend taking the coastal A92 south of Stonehaven, passing the dramatic Dunnotter Castle, sitting precariously on a rocky promontory, and enjoy the magnificent coastal views. Kincardineshire would give us the Fettercairn Distillery situated in the delightful village of that name and only a few miles from the well-regarded James Braid course at Edzell. Angus, whether the ancient county or the modern province, starts just north of Montrose and includes the old county town of Forfar, the City of Brechin and Arbroath, scene of the famous Declaration of 1320, a letter sent to the Pope on behalf of King Robert 1st asserting the independence of the Kingdom of Scotland. The likes of Forfar, Brechin City and Arbroath are often best known for their football teams and Forfar was of course involved in the mythical football match when they defeated East Fife 5-4. This tongue-twister result, made famous by Eric Morcambe, (East Fife 4 Forfar 5) never actually happened though it has almost done so on two occasions; in 1964 Forfar won 5-4 at home to East Fife (Forfar 5 East Fife 4 – not quite as good!) and they did win a penalty shoot-out at East Fife by that score following a one-all draw in 2008. I apologise to overseas readers for this indulgence in what is a typically British nonsense. Distilleries in Angus once included two in Montrose (Glenesk and Lochside) and two in nearby Brechin (North Port and Glencadam). Of these, only Glencadam survives and looks secure as part of the small Angus Dundee Distillers company which also owns the Tomintoul distillery. Plans for a visitor centre have also just been approved by the local council.

However, it was the arrival of a new whisky distillery on the Arbikie estate which caught my attention and allowed me to re-visit what is a golden stretch of links golf on the Angus coast. There are four courses in particular: Montrose Old Links, the 5th oldest in the world, Panmure at Barry, Monifieth and Carnoustie, the well-known Open Championship venue. In all, this 25-mile stretch of coastline has some nine courses.

To me it was a choice between Montrose and Panmure and fate found me playing in competitions at each within a couple of weeks of each other.

Montrose sits on the coast and alongside Montrose Basin, which is a tidal sea loch and the largest inland salt-water lagoon in the UK, an important habitat for mute swans and other birdlife. It has an exceptionally wide High Street and some impressive old buildings. The golf courses are old, traditional links and like St. Andrews (and indeed Monifieth and Carnoustie) are owned by a Links Trust and played over by different clubs. At one time there were five different clubs playing over the links, a structure not conducive to there being consistent investment in the course and the clubhouse facilities. Montrose now has two as Royal Montrose and Montrose Mercantile have recently amalgamated to form (you've guessed it) The Royal Montrose Mercantile Club. Montrose Caledonia remains a separate club. The amalgamation will allow two clubhouses which had seen better days to be replaced by one new upgraded one, something which is badly needed for both members and visitors alike. It is to be hoped that it also facilitates continued investment in maintaining the course.

The Old Course is called the 1562 Course although there seems little detail available on what sort of 'course' existed in that era. Rather like at Dornoch and St. Andrews it is simply known that some form of golf was played in this area at that time. While Old Tom Morris was involved in designing a layout in 1888, today's layout is a result of work by Willie Park Junior in 1903 and completed by Harry Colt in 1913. Colt was also responsible for the second course, The Broomfield, in the 1920s.

I had last played Montrose over twenty years' ago and my memory was of the early holes in the dunes by the sea being more interesting than the later holes which lie on flatter terrain inland. While this is not an unreasonable summary, I was pleasantly surprised by the inland flatter holes which are not without interest and certainly not without challenge.

Like all good layouts there are many changes in direction which require you to calculate what the wind is doing. The first hole takes you from the clubhouse out to the sea with a gently rising fairway to a green on top of the dune. At the second hole you encounter Montrose's biggest challenge where much of the fairway has been removed by coastal erosion. There is some debate as to the reasons behind this though it seems likely that there are other local factors at play beyond simply rising sea levels – nearby river dredging and other coastal protection schemes have probably moved the problem towards the golf course. A redesign of the hole was undertaken by Martin Hawtree taking your drive slightly inland with a gentle dog-leg back along the coast to the original green. It is still a very good hole and the beach on the right remains intimidating. The 3rd is a memorable Par 3 to what looks like a small target. There follows a series of holes which take you broadly along the coast and back until 10 which starts the section of the course which lies on the flatter land inside the dunes. With gorse in abundance and subtle shaping these have plenty of character. The long Par 5 15th brings you back to the dunes where there is a tough long Par 3 with a difficult green followed by 17 which requires a delicate second shot to catch the green slightly raised on the side of a dune. 18, in traditional links style, takes you back towards the town and the clubhouses.

It had been the same length of time since I had played Panmure. Indeed, this book is full of courses which I was playing for the second time -it was true at Fortrose and Rosemarkie and Cruden Bay and also applies to Scotscraig in Chapter 7. I had two main memories: an excellent clubhouse and a course with a slightly boring start and finish and an excellent middle. My memory proved to be fairly accurate though this time, rather like at Montrose, I found the difference between the starting and finishing holes and the middle section less of a contrast. It is true that the middle section of the course is laid out on a more pleasing area of links with elevation changes and probably includes the best holes but I didn't find the other holes nearer the clubhouse disappointing.

Let's start with the clubhouse as it has to be one of Scotland's best. Clubs which have been able to retain their original clubhouse buildings are lucky as generally they have more character and this is certainly the case at Panmure. The club was originally founded in 1845 and played over 9 holes in the Monifieth area but as that became congested, it moved in 1899 to the current site and the clubhouse dates from then. It is quite large with a huge bar area looking out over the course enabling members and visitors to mingle pleasingly. The dining room is also a good big room with high ceilings and has recently been refurbished. The style of the clubhouse was apparently modelled on that of the Royal Calcutta Golf Club as a result of the strong links between nearby Dundee and India through the jute industry. I think the clubhouse experience is an important part of a day's golf. In Scotland, at the premium end, Prestwick and Muirfield deliver it memorably but there are many great golf courses and even great golf clubs which don't quite do so – Montrose would currently be an example. I think I awarded Moray as my favourite clubhouse in my first book. Other favourites in Scotland are Western Gailes and Royal Aberdeen but Panmure would be right up there. In England I think some my favourites would be Royal St. George's, Tandridge and Denham while Royal Porthcawl in Wales must also get a mention.

Old Tom Morris, as usual, was consulted on the layout and then James Braid suggested a few modifications which were made in 1922. While I think the contrast between the holes near the clubhouse and the others can be overdone, there is no doubt that the most memorable ones are in the middle section. The 4th is a Par 4 dogleg with an awkward raised green and 5 is a classic links Par 3. The most famous hole is probably 6 which sets up pleasingly from the tee but requires an accurate drive between the low-lying dunes and then plays to the left and slightly uphill to a smallish green. Lurking front right is 'Hogan's bunker'. Ben Hogan, on his only visit to the UK, won the 1953 Open Championship at nearby Carnoustie and spent two weeks beforehand practising at Panmure to acclimatise to links conditions and to the smaller UK ball – the US and UK balls were not standardised until the 1970s. Hogan liked the hole and suggested that a pot bunker there would add to the challenge. The 7th is a long Par 4 and plays in the opposite direction and on the day I played was into the wind which was a cold one coming from the north-east. With a prevailing south-westerly this would usually be a short respite from playing into the wind on the front 9. The 8th is a narrow but quite short Par 4 while the Par 3 9th plays across the course to a two-tier green. The 12th is the end of the course where the green is over a large burn and surrounding rough area. 13 then heads for home. The Par 5 14th was particularly tough the day I played – the green has recently been re-sited and there is no respite with 15 being a 234 yard Par 3 – almost impossible to reach into the wind. Three par 4s take you back to the clubhouse – 16 is probably the best of these and while they don't have some of the character of the earlier holes, they remain testing.

You can't call Panmure a spectacular location. The course is not set against the coast – the same is true of Carnoustie and Monifieth - and the scenery is pleasant rather than dramatic. It is more akin to the Lancashire coast courses than say East Lothian or the drama of Dornoch and Brora. But it is a true links golf of the highest quality and while Montrose's seaside location is perhaps prettier, Panmure's wonderful clubhouse gets my vote.

The Arbikie estate has been farmed by four generations of the Stirling family and today, three brothers, John, Iain and David, have diversified into distilling. The Stirling family had originally been farmers on the west coast but had moved to Angus in the 1920s. They claim to have records of distilling on their land in the 18th century (they use 1794 in the branding) and wish to re-create a local 'field to bottle' proposition. They actually started with vodka distilled from their own potatoes and soon followed up with gin. Whisky production began in 2015 with barley grown in their own fields and malted locally at Boorts in Montrose. Unlike many start-ups, they don't intend to release malt whisky as soon as possible (3 years) and intend to wait until at least ten. Meanwhile the business will sell its vodka and gin as well as a single grain whisky. Confusingly, the Scotch Whisky Regulations don't require 'single grain' whisky to be made from a 'single' grain – the 'single' refers to the distillery – and so a combination of any grains can be used, whereas a 'single malt' requires only malted barley. Arbikie 1794 Highland Rye whisky (a mixed mash of unmalted rye, unmalted wheat and malted barley) is matured for three years in charred American oak and is described as the world's first rye Scotch for over 100 years. I have a number of observations about it. With the many start-ups in the industry, each has to seek differentiation and this is certainly that. The product is very distinctive, rich dark with a strong rye flavour. For me it is more a whisky to be used with a mixer as I don't think it has the rounded smoothness of a well-aged single malt. What is fascinating from a business point of view is the price they are selling the product for; the current website contains three Highland Rye releases selling at between £95 and £250 for a limited edition. This is impressive. It will be interesting to see how they position their single malt when it is released.

Whatever the characteristics of the individual product lines there is a powerful overarching proposition of 'field to bottle' combined with sustainability and provenance. Sustainability is obviously something which many distilleries, and indeed businesses in all sectors, are now making central to their strategy – we will see it at NcNean on the west coast in my third Scottish book. In some ways, however, sustainability will become what in marketing circles is called a 'qualifier' rather than a 'differentiator' for a business, so more important for Arbikie is the local 'field to bottle' angle – they grow what they distil. This applies to everything from the potatoes for the vodka to the grain and the botanicals for their gins. This is a powerful statement and is clear to see from a visit to the distillery which opened to the public in early 2022. In fact, I had the privilege of being the very first outside visitor. My visit had been postponed as the opening of the new visitor centre and café was delayed because they were waiting for a licence from the council (I don't know the details so will resist the temptation to express frustration at how slow bureaucracy can so often stifle enterprise). The licence still had not come through on the re-fixed date but they agreed that I could come and look around on an informal basis. Amusingly they got confirmation that the licence had been issued during my visit.

A Highland Cow greets visitors to the Arbikie Distillery

The distillery is situated high up on a hillside looking out to sea over Lunan Bay – it's a glorious view. You turn off the A92 about four miles south of Montrose and drive through the estate amidst the crops in the fields which grow the raw materials for the distillery. You are greeted by a herd of highland cows at the main gate. In this sense there is an immediate understanding of the field to bottle concept – the fields, literally surround the distillery which has been built around an old cattle barn and farm buildings. It is now an impressive structure sitting proudly on the hillside and inside the design is arresting, a large airy space with a modern but rustic feel. It's designed not just for tours but as a café and bar to attract both tourist and local trade, serving soups, sandwiches, salads and homemade cakes. I had a coffee which was exceptional – I'm fussy about my coffee and this was as good a coffee as I have had anywhere. I always think the quality of the coffee is a signal of the quality of the other offerings so I am confident the rest of the offerings will be good too.

There has been much debate in the whisky industry about the importance or otherwise of 'terroir'. In wine, the soil conditions and climate as well as the grape variety are crucial in influencing the end product as much as the process. In some areas, whether the vine is on a south-facing or north-facing slope can be all important. Arbikie can trace all their raw material, be it barley, other grains or potatoes, not only to their estate but to particular fields on their estate. Indeed, in the distillery is a wooden wall-mounted map of all the fields, each of which is named. This is impressive traceability, an increasingly popular proposition in the food industry. I saw it also at The Owl Distillery in Belgium where, again, the grain was grown in fields surrounding the distillery. The question is whether it matters in the production of whisky; does the barley from one part of the estate make better whisky than that from another area? As I have said before, in my view it doesn't matter whether it matters. Whisky thrives on mystery and adding another element of mystery can only add to its appeal.

Three main tours are offered, each an hour long, and each focusing on one product area: the whisky experience, the gin experience and the cocktail experience. This is not just a whisky distillery; gin and vodka are core parts of the offering, not just cash-generating extras. There are a number of different lines of gin and vodka and both ranges include a *Nadar* variety which is distilled from peas and therefore claims to be the first 'climate positive' gin and vodka. *Nadar* means 'nature' in Gaelic. Peas and other legumes have always been known to have an important role in crop rotation and it is the reduced use of nitrogen and recycling of waste into animal feed on the farm which supports the 'climate positive' claim. This makes an important statement about the business. However, I don't think the Scotch Whisky Regulations will allow a 'whisky' to be distilled from peas – a 'single legume' whisky is not yet an approved category!

A few words about the gin. Again, they grow the botanicals on the estate, mainly in polytunnels to overcome the Scottish climate which would not otherwise be ideal for the likes of lemongrass and lime leaves. I bought a bottle of Kirsty's Gin and, while I am no gin expert, I found it one of the best gins I had ever tasted. It is very smooth and distinctive and named after its creator, Kirsty Black, Arbikie's Master Distiller. Kirsty is an excellent example of another pleasing trend in the industry: an increasing number of women involved in all aspects of distillery businesses. Kirsty had an interest in home brewing which led her to study brewing and distilling at the International Centre for Brewing and Distilling at Heriot Watt University in Edinburgh whence she was asked by the Stirling family to become involved in setting up the new distillery.

There is much to admire about the Arbikie business: local, modern, innovative yet with a genuine heritage. It has thought about its story and it is a good one. The scale is small, though more than artisan, and the price unashamedly premium. It should do well.

The tough uphill Par 3 14th hole on the Queen's Course at Gleneagles

The view from the 18th tee on the Queen's Course at Gleneagles with the lovely Ochil Hills in the background

CHAPTER SIX

PERTHSHIRE REVISITED

'What earthly good is golf? Life is stern and life is earnest. We live in a practical age. All round us we see foreign competition making itself unpleasant. And we spend our time playing golf!'

P.G. Wodehouse (1881-1975)
The Clicking of Cuthbert

PERTHSHIRE IS BIG enough for me not to apologise for including it again in this second book on Scotland. I hadn't played Gleneagles since I was a teenager and wanted to return. Meanwhile there was still much whisky to explore. Perthshire is the home of many famous Blended Scotch brands: Bells at Blair Atholl, Dewars at Aberfeldy and until recently The Famous Grouse at Glenturret. The nearest distillery to Gleneagles is actually Tullabardine at Blackford, home of the less well-known Highland Cream though in the 1970s it was one of the leading Scotch export brands.

There have been many interesting ownership changes. While Bell's remains part of the Diageo blended portfolio, Dewars is now owned by Bacardi and with both Glenturret and Tullabardine, we again encounter French ownership. The former was sold by The Famous Grouse's owners in 2019 to the French luxury-brands company, Lalique, while the latter had enjoyed a complicated ownership history, being bought from Whyte and Mackay by a consortium in 2003 which sold it to the French wine producer, Picard, in 2011. Both sites are worth a visit.

Gleneagles, rather like Cruden Bay, started out as a resort on the back of the development of the railways. It was the vision of Donald Matheson, General Manager of the Caledonian Railway Company who developed plans for a hotel and golf courses in 1913. The war delayed construction but in 1919 James Braid was commissioned to design the two golf courses with the construction of the hotel re-starting in 1922.

Gleneagles is one of two 'resort locations' which I have included in this book, rather against my instincts. But I think that there is enough relevant history to justify it being on your 'must play' list in Scotland. There are three courses: The King's and The Queen's, both Braid designs from the 1920s, and the PGA Centenary Course, built to attract big tournaments to the venue and which has held both a Ryder Cup and a Solheim Cup. I have never played The PGA Centenary course just as I have never played The Belfry or Celtic Manor and to be honest none of them are high on my list of courses I want to play. To me they are designed for professional tournament play and seldom present a fun and engaging type of golfing experience, especially for mid-handicappers like me. It is true that some new courses now present a large number of tee options to allow shorter hitters to play but for me they don't hold the same appeal of many lesser-known older courses. The turf at The PGA Centenary is also quite different from the older courses, being built on lower ground so it does not have the same 'heathland' look and feel and therefore is not conducive to the type of golf which I enjoy the most.

I am going to suggest that rather than playing The King's Course, you should enjoy The Queen's instead. I will also make a claim about The Queen's Course – it is the second best 'second course' anywhere in the UK and Ireland and looking at the rankings it is generally agreed to be superior to other better-known candidates such as Wentworth East, The Berkshire Blue, Walton Heath New, St Andrews New, Ballyliffin Old, Ballybunion Cashen or Gullane No. 2. Which is the best second course? Surely Sunningdale New but I am sure you can argue otherwise - indeed some might say it is Sunningdale Old!

As well as being the only venue which has held both a Ryder Cup and a Solheim Cup, Gleneagles has a role in the history of the former. The origin of the Cup dates back to the 1920s and was the inspiration of Samuel Ryder, a seed merchant from St. Albans. He was a member of both the Veralum Golf Club in St Albans and Camb Down Golf Club in Dorset where he regularly went on holidays with his family. This was an era when American golfers were beginning what became a long period of ascendancy in the world of golf – the Great Triumvirate (Braid, Vardon and Taylor), who had dominated pre-war, were ageing and since the famous victory of Francis Ouimet in the US Open of 1913, interest in the US had taken off. Ryder felt that there should be a match between American and British golfers and, in conjunction with his brother, James, arranged some informal contests. In 1924 a fourball challenge between Abe Mitchell and George Duncan of Britain against the well-known Americans, Walter Hagan and McDonald Smith, took place at the St George's Hill and Oxhey clubs and the following year a singles challenge was arranged between Mitchell and Jim Barnes, the popular Cornish-born American. But most people point to a more formal 'International Match' which took place at Wentworth in June the following year, as the real start of what was to become the Ryder Cup. The first match to be known as the Ryder Cup was played at Worcester Country Club in Massachusetts in 1927. However, perhaps the real foundations were laid as early as early as June 1921 when an 'International Challenge' match was held comprising five foursomes and ten singles at the new Gleneagles course between the professionals of the two countries. The American team included both Walter Hagan and Jock Hutchison while the UK team boasted not only all of the Great Triumvirate but also Ted Ray and George Duncan. For the record the UK won 9-3 (halved matches were awarded no points).

The reason for choosing The Queen's was that I had never played it and that many people I know had said to me 'actually, I prefer the Queen's'. There are probably two or three reasons for this. While both courses enjoy the same glorious backdrop, the Queen's is probably the prettier of the two with its undulating topography, small woods, copses and lochans. It is Perthshire in miniature. Secondly there is a huge variety of hole types – no two holes are similar and it is a course that is easy to remember for that reason. Finally, it is probably a little easier than The King's and that often helps enjoyment. Golf is for enjoying and it is not always about testing yourself on the hardest courses, playing off the back tees. Try playing shorter courses, treat yourself to the front tees. The PGA course is 6,800 yards off the white tees, The King's just under 6,500 and the Queen's just under 6,000. I guess it depends on what you want but I do feel that too many golfers play courses off tees which are not designed for their level of ability and thus miss out on enjoying themselves as much as they could.

There are so many distinctive holes on The Queen's that it is difficult to single out a few. I would say that the back 9 is better than the front 9 (or was that because I played it a lot better?) but another observation is that I think the best holes are probably the shorter Par 4s – again this might reflect my preference as someone who no longer hits a long ball. The 355-yard 4th is both a pretty hole and one which requires great accuracy both off the tee and into the trickily positioned green with bunkers at the front and a steep bank off to the left. I also liked the difficult Par 3 5th which requires a firm shot to a slightly hidden green – well, I would like it as I got a 2. On the back 9, 10 is a great hole playing downhill to a green hidden left in a hollow behind some hillocks – you really have to play into it from the right-hand side of the fairway. 11 is a short, innocent-looking Par 4 of just over 300 yards but, again, a well-positioned drive to the right will make life much easier. 12 has a dramatic downhill slope halfway along the fairway – it is probably easier to play your second in from the top of it so it is best for long hitters to lay up a bit. Two consecutive Par 3s follow, prettily positioned by a gloriously tranquil lochan (a small loch), the first shortish and flat and the second longish and sharply uphill to a narrow two-tiered green. 15 is then a dangerous short Par 4 of only 252 yards – do you dare try and drive to the small green? This is the type of golf I like. I also liked the 200-yard Par 3 17th which sets up beautifully from the tee looking down to a green nestled alongside a ridge with the panorama of the Ochil Hills in the distance. A long raking fade will allow you to run the ball into the deep narrow green – well, it allowed me to, and I holed the putt for my second 2 of the round. No wonder I like The Queen's! 18 is also visually exciting, played from a high tee down towards the clubhouse with a tree on the left, the main hazard if your drive is not correctly positioned on the fairway.

The golf here is inspiring – the variety of holes, the ability to bump and run, the Perthshire scenery, the wonderfully kept course. Mention should also be made of a high-quality halfway hut which is worth frequenting after putting out on the 10th. In fact, while Gleneagles obviously does not have a 'members' club' feel, the experience for the visiting golfer is a very good one. The facilities are top class, the welcome friendly and the atmosphere relaxed. You get balls to use on the practice range as part of the green fee which is how it should be. Yes, it's expensive - the green fee is high but not exorbitant and the same can be said for the price of the food whether you eat in the restaurant or the bar which both look out over the courses.

Glenturret is located in a peaceful valley a few miles north of Crieff. It has an 'off the beaten track' feel to it as you drive along a narrow road to reach it. The origins date back to 1775 when smugglers established a small illicit distillery called Hosh. A legal distillery called Glenturret was started nearby in 1826 but this was decommissioned and the name Glenturret taken on by Hosh. Production ceased after the Great War and was not re-started until a new owner bought it in the 1950s. During the 1980s, Remy Cointreau made their first venture into the Scotch industry, purchasing the distillery and opening a visitor centre which was quite rare at the time. Remy then sold it in 1990 to Highland Distillers, a major distilling group at the time which became part of the Edrington Group in 1999. It became the home of the Famous Grouse brand and a new visitor centre, The Famous Grouse Experience, was opened in 1992. The Famous Grouse brand was first registered by the well-known Perthshire family, Gloag in 1897. It was at first known as just 'The Grouse' with 'Famous Grouse' being first registered in 1906. By 1980 it had become the biggest selling blended brand in Scotland and was awarded a Royal Warrant in 1984. It also became the leading brand in Scandanavia. In recent years it has continued to be heavily marketed with many premium expressions and blended malts. Yet, Glenturret can no longer really be seen as the home of the brand, as Edrington sold the Glenturret distillery to a joint venture between the Swiss-born American-based industrialist Hansjorg Wyss and the French Lalique Group in in 2019, moving the marketing office to Glasgow and closing the Famous Grouse Visitor Centre. While the distillery is likely to still provide malted product for the brand, the new owners' focus is to develop the Glenturret malt brand and invest in the production site. The Lalique Group describes itself as 'a niche player in the luxury goods industry with an international presence and a global reach'. With its focus on 'perfumes, cosmetics, crystal glass and jewellery', whisky will be just a niche within this niche but again this emphasizes the international appeal and image of premium malt Scotch whisky.

They have retained the visitor centre which now boasts a shop – the Lalique Boutique - featuring products and brands from the Lalique group – glassware, jewellery, perfumes, art and interior design items as well as whisky and whisky-related items. It is slightly incongruous to find a shop selling such a range of luxury items in rural Perthshire. It feels more like a store you might encounter in Bond Street in London or the Boulevard Haussman in Paris but I guess the site attracts many customers with a high disposable income. The nearby Gleneagles Hotel perhaps offers a clue – you will certainly need some disposable income to stay there – and a special Glenturret release for the famous hotel has been produced. There is also a Michelin-starred restaurant and a bar at the distillery – the tasting menu is £150 which may sound a lot but is the same as the green fee at Gleneagles. It depends what you want to spend your money on. With a top chef and a notable wine cellar from wine estates around the world owned by both Lalique's Chairman and Founder Silvio Denz and Hansjorg Wyss (Bordeaux, Tuscany, Catalonia and California, so plenty of choice) I'm sure you will not be disappointed. The £150 for the food though may just be a rather minor part of your budget to eat there. While there are some wines for around £50 a bottle you might be tempted by a 2001 Petrus at £2,900 per bottle or even a 2013 Grand Cru Cotes de Nuits at £5,800 per bottle! I didn't sample the restaurant but had a reasonably priced, delicious coffee – the second top-class coffee I had enjoyed at a whisky distillery after the notable one at Arbikie. I'm increasingly of the view that those who pay attention to serving a good coffee are likely to show the same care and attention to detail in making whisky.

All this says so much about whisky. Whether it's a wealthy industrialist with an interest in the fine things in life or a luxury goods business, whisky has become an essential part of an international premium brands portfolio. Previously this could have been achieved by working with an independent bottler but increasingly owning an old distillery is the favoured option. A Scotch malt whisky distillery has become a natural bedfellow to wine estates in St. Emilion or the Napa Valley. And while certain limited wines can fetch what look like extraordinary prices so can exclusive whiskies. In marketing circles, we would refer to it as a 'super-premium' sector of the market and the existence of these exclusive, seemingly ridiculously priced products, is a sign of a healthy market.

Glenturret, Scotland's oldest whisky distillery – even older than Fortrose and Rosemarkie Golf Club!

The distillery is receiving much investment but remains relatively small and traditional in its process. Capacity is to be increased slightly but already the Glenturret range has been relaunched in a new bottle which unsurprisingly has a designer glass-decanter look to it. Indeed, there is also a premium release called The Trinity Provenance which is packaged in a Lalique Crystal Decanter and sells for £9,800 per bottle on the website which makes the Cotes de Nuits look like a bargain. The new ranges were made possible as the purchase of the distillery included a lot of maturing stock, allowing the new owners to get their ranges to market quickly. You can buy Glenturret malts from 10-year-old to 30-year-old, peat smoked and a Triple Wood. In 2021 a release was produced celebrating the 60th anniversary of the E Type Jaguar, reflecting how Lalique like to match with other premium brands. The distillery tour is conventional and emphasizes the distillery's history, a traditional approach to process and the slow distillation.

The link with wine is even more overt at Tullibardine which is owned directly by a wine company. Picard Vins et Spiriteux actually made their first foray into the industry by buying the Muirheads and Highland Queen blended brands from Glenmorangie in 2008. France remains the biggest export market for blended Scotch (it's second to the USA for malt Scotch) and has the world's highest per capita Scotch consumption which explains the strong involvement of French businesses in the industry. Again, the ultimate aim was to have a distillery and Tullabardine was bought in 2011. Picard is a French family business but as well, as high-end French wine domains producing Chassagne-Montrachet, Condrieu, Chateauneuf-du-Pape and Sancerre, they have brands of Cognac, Rum (from the French island of Réunion), Tequila and premium beers.

The location isn't quite as quaint as Glenturret because the distillery sits alongside the A9 so doesn't enjoy Glenturret's tranquillity. Tullibardine traces its history back to the 15th century but as a location for brewing rather than distilling. James IV of Scotland granted the brewery a royal charter in 1503 but distilling didn't start until 1947 when the owner, a local architect, William Delmé-Evans founded the distillery. It went through a number of ownership changes before becoming part of Whyte & Mackay who mothballed it in 1994. It was sold to a consortium in 2003 when production restarted then the current owners bought it in 2011. The malt production from the distillery had mainly been used as part of the blended brands and the stock had been held in old tired casks unsuitable for the production of a single malt. This required much of the stock to be re-casked, an expensive and time-consuming operation. It seems, however, that as a private business, they are taking the long view and are investing accordingly. There is a smart visitor centre and shop with tours and on-site bottling is to be added to what is quite a large site.

Now as well as continuing to market and sell their substantial blended brands, Muirheads and Highland Cream, ranges of malts are appearing. The Signature range contains the main 15-year-old Bourbon cask product as well as a 20 and 25-year-old while there are also Sauternes, Burgundy and sherry cask finishes. The limited edition 'The Murray' range, named after the 2nd Marquess of Tullabardine, William Murray, a famous Jacobite who fought at the Battle of Sheriffmuir during the first Jacobite Rebellion of 1715, also contains various cask finishes while there are other even more premium ranges. Again, much investment in premium products for an international audience.

One other note about Tullabardine: it was the distillery which initially worked with the innovative Scottish Biofuel business, Celtic Renewables, which in conjunction with Napier University developed a process to take waste material from the whisky distilling process (draff and pot ale) to create biofuel. It is called the ABE (Acetone-Buthenol-Ethanol) Fermentation Process and the business has gone on to secure investment in a large production facility at Grangemouth. There are many positive stories on how the whisky industry is reacting to the challenges of climate change.

Within 15 miles of each other in the Perthshire countryside, here are two French businesses which have relatively recently purchased old Scottish distilleries and are now investing in premium ranges of Scotch malts for an international luxury market. As a proud Scot, and a marketer by background who understands the importance and opportunity of having a unique product to sell, I find this exciting and uplifting. Scotland has had at different times a reputation for industries like textiles, oil, ship-building and financial services but all these are subject to global pressures and can ultimately always potentially be produced more cheaply elsewhere. Scotch whisky can only be produced in Scotland and the authentic Scottish golf experience can only be had in Scotland. As long as the proprietors of these unique assets – Scotland's whisky distilleries and Scotland's golf courses – nurture them, their futures offer exciting opportunities for the people of Scotland.

Traditional style wooden washbacks at the modern Lindores Distillery

The clubhouse at Scotscraig oozes charm and history

CHAPTER SEVEN

FIFE REVISITED

'Freedom and whisky gang the gather.'

Robert Burns (1759-1796)
Scottish poet

I HAVE PREVIOUSLY suggested that Fife is to golf was what Speyside is to whisky, the spiritual home. This is not just because of St Andrews, to many the acknowledged home of the game, but because it boasts so many great courses across the 'Kingdom'. I wanted on this occasion to feature one outside of St Andrews but this does not narrow the field that much. Along Fife's southern coast Lundin and Leven Links are classic links courses and clubs with distinguished histories. James Braid was born on this coast at Earlsferry next to Elie, or to give the club its full name, The Golf House Club, Elie, where you will find a delightful, slightly eccentric, links of 16 Par 4s and just two Par 3s. Those who have played there will remember its iconic periscope which protrudes from the starter's hut to give a view over the hill and down the first fairway, allowing players to know when the group in front is safely out of range. The periscope was salvaged from HMS Excalibur in 1966 and presented to the club by a member.

Further round the coast you come to the home of The Crail Golfing Society, even older than Elie, which now boasts two courses; the Balcomie links laid out by Old Tom Morris in 1895 and the new Craighead links. Next there is Kingsbarns, one of the best known and greatest of modern links courses, laid out by Mark Parsinen and Kyle Phillips on land which is reputed to have been occupied by a golf course many decades before. The success of Kingsbarns made it a model for many subsequent new links courses, a new course but one designed with the traditional game in mind. One of the newest of these is the Dumbarnie Links, opened in 2020, not far away from Elie which is getting good reviews. Fife also has some good inland courses, perhaps the most notable being Ladybank of which the original nine was designed by Old Tom with a second nine being added in 1962 by Laurie Auchterlonie Jr, son of Willie Auchterlonie, the winner of The Open at St Andrews in 1893. North Fife is less well-known and perhaps not as obviously attractive. However, about ten miles north of St Andrews there is another ancient club with a distinguished history but one that undeservedly gets missed out in many a golf tour of Fife: Scotscraig at Tayport.

Having said that Speyside is really the spiritual home of whisky (I like the idea of whisky having a 'spiritual' home), there is in fact a case to be made for Fife. One of the earliest written references to whisky was in the Exchequer Roll of 1494 which named Brother John Cor of Lindores Abbey on the north coast of Fife as being commissioned by King James IV to turn '8 bolls of malt into acqua vitae'. Lindores Abbey had been founded in 1191 by David, Earl of Huntingdon, the brother of King William 1st of Scotland. Known as William the Lion, his forty-nine-year reign was the longest of any Scottish king before the 'Union of the Crowns' in 1603. He liked to live at Falkland Palace not far from Lindores. He was a great supporter of the Scottish church and also founded Arbroath Abbey. Lindores Abbey, as with Arbroath and others in Scotland, was occupied by the Tironensian Order of monks from France and it may be that the art of distilling had been learned from there. As well as their scholarly and religious devotions, the Tironensians were known for their horticultural and medicinal skills and saw manual labour as an important part of their remit. The abbey became well known for its orchards growing apples, pears and plums.

The abbey lies just outside the town of Newburgh. Like Tayport, it is not as well-known as its counterparts on the southern coast and less affluent, so the decision by Drew and Helen Mackenzie Smith to invest in a new distillery alongside the ancient abbey was an enormous boon for the town. The abbey had belonged to the family for over a century, having been bought by Drew's grandfather in 1913, but Drew and Helen had worked mainly in the high-end hospitality industry and it was only when reading about the story of Friar John Cor and the Exchequer Roll of 1494 that the idea of setting up a distillery was formed. A £10-million project supported by European investors was started in 2013 but building a distillery next to such a historic building clearly was subject to sensitive planning issues. Also, excavation of the adjacent land, the site of an old farm steading, soon revealed more historic artefacts and the site became the scene of a full-scale archaeological dig which delayed the opening of the distillery.

The architecturally stunning visitor centre and distillery opened in 2017. The building oozes quality using local materials, wood from Denmylne and stone from Clatchard Quarry. There is a very special feel to the place from the moment you walk in. Tours can be pre-booked and private tours arranged as required while the space is also set up for hire for private events. The distillery itself is on the top floor designed to take in views both of the old abbey grounds which surround the building but also over the Tay Estuary to Dundee and inland to the Fife hills. Here there is farmland from where they are sourcing their barley while they are also constructing a purpose-built dunnage warehouse on the site.

What about the product? Another quirk of the new distillery is that the Lowland/Highland whisky regions dividing line is the road which dissects the site; the main part of the original abbey is in the Highlands while the new distillery is in the Lowlands – something similar is the case at Glengoyne in the west of Scotland. The objective is to produce a lightly peated Lowland style whisky, a Lowland whisky with hints of Highland characteristics perhaps. Like many start-ups, they were fortunate to work with the late Jim Swan and the approach to the distilling process reflects this. Being a small-scale operation, quality is central to everything. The fermentation time in the traditional wooden washbacks is long, while the one-wash still and two-spirit stills are designed for maximum copper contact. As well as using local Laureate barley they are examining traditional forms of yeast. The water comes from a borehole which would have served the abbey back in the 15th century. While malting is currently from Muntons, they are considering bringing that in house. Finally, as ever, there are the casks and here, as with any new distiller, they are experimenting with bourbon, red wine barriques from Spain and also ones from Australia. They believe the long fermentation time will help speed maturation and they have installed heating in part of the dunnage warehouse for the same purpose. Certainly, reading early reviews of their initial releases, the experts believe that Lindores is delivering a quality product.

Instead of producing gin to aid cashflow, as most new distilleries have done, Lindores is making an Aqua Vitae with their new make spirit. The spirit is infused with a blend of herbs and spices including lemon verbena, douglas fir and sweet cicely all foraged from within the Abbey grounds. I tasted it on my tour and it was certainly very pleasant and fragrant – whether it has the same market potential as gin, I'm not sure, but it is something different and it is part of the brand story. They are planting a new orchard in the grounds reflecting the abbey's heritage and plan also to use the fruit in their distillate.

It was only a few years ago when starting to write my first book that I pointed out how strange it was that there were so few distilleries in Fife. Daftmill was, at the time, the pioneer and Kingsbarns and Eden Mill have followed. The potential link with the tourist attraction of golf in Fife was obvious and Kingsbarns was the first to do this overtly. Lindores Abbey is the latest new entrant and its impressive visitor centre should attract whisky and golfing tourists alike. As we will see in Edinburgh, often one new distillery attracts another and the competition benefits all. Lindores Abbey with its distinctive story and heritage looks set to take its place among the list of successful new distillery start-ups.

It takes about a half an hour to drive from Lindores to Tayport. You pass the southern end of the Tay Bridge which emphasizes that this area of Fife is much closer to Dundee than Edinburgh and that will be reflected in Scotscraig's membership. The golf club sits to the south of Tayport on the edge of Tentsmuir, a magnificent National Nature Reserve comprising large areas of forest, the Morton Lochs, three reed-fringed small lochs which provide shelter and protection for many rare birds and animals, and the Headwell Sands, a shifting landscape of dunes and sands which is an important habitat for seals and migrating birds. It is no coincidence that visits to historic golf courses so often brings us to nearby nature reserves; great golf courses require the same type of soil and landscape preferred by migrating birds and nature generally. I think of Silloth and Southerness on the Solway Firth, the sand dunes of Balmedie and Forvie in Aberdeenshire, or Fäno Links by the Wadden Sea off Denmark and Falsterbo in southern Sweden. The best golf courses are the ones that don't compete with nature but are part of it.

Scotscraig's clubhouse may be slightly showing its age but that is because it is still the original building which was built in 1896. It is packed full of golfing memorabilia and is well worth a mooch around. This is a local club proud of its distinguished history, claiming to be the 13th-oldest in the world – that's two older than Fortrose and Rosemarkie. I am not sure who holds the definitive list of oldest golf clubs as I don't think the individual claims of each club are entirely consistent. I don't think it matters and Scotscraig is definitely old, having been founded in 1817 by members of The St Andrews Society of Golfers which was later to become the R&A so it has very close links with the heart of the Scottish golfing establishment. In 1818 a competition was played for The Gold Medal and this is still played for today, one of the oldest competitions in golf. Despite this, the club, or at least the course, had a difficult history during the 19th century with evidence that the course was ploughed up in the 1830s and the Gold Medal being held at times at other courses such as St Andrews and Montrose. In 1887 the land on which the course stood was purchased by Admiral Maitland-Dougall and Old Tom Morris was involved in creating a course of 9 holes. This was followed by the new clubhouse being built in 1896. The first hole today is called 'Admiral' in his memory. The course was extended to 18 holes in 1904 but today's layout is largely the work of James Braid in 1923.

The course is something of a hybrid of heathland and links. It is some distance from the sea so doesn't immediately have a links feel but its characteristics are distinctly linksy at times. It is not a surprise that since 1984 it has been used frequently as an Open Championship qualifier.

Some golf courses and layouts lend themselves to remembering each hole better than others. I generally find it difficult to remember every hole on a course if I have only played it once. I make a point after playing a course for the first time of trying to 'play my way around' it afterwards in my head. It's funny how sometimes you forget some holes and have to consult the website or scorecard for the course layout in order to remember. Playing a course for a second time is usually enough for me to be able to remember every hole.

Indeed, if you are looking for ways of getting to sleep, I recommend walking through your latest round, shot by shot, whether at a new course or a familiar one. I often look to award myself 'shot of the round'. You start by coming up with a short list – maybe the 7 iron to a tricky pin position at the 3rd or perhaps the tee shot on the long Par 3 10th which found the middle of the green. Or maybe it was that thirty-foot putt on 17 that lipped out. I'm generally asleep before I decide. It is one of the great things about golf – even within a bad round there will usually be some rewarding shots to savour. Professional sportsmen are taught to 'focus on the positives' and we amateurs should do the same. Yet again golf delivers a lesson for life generally.

The view over the ancient abbey gardens from the upper floor still-house at Lindores Distillery

Other variants of this insomniac's pastime are to choose your favourite composite golf course -perhaps the best 18 holes across the Open venues or the best 18 of the famous '3Ws'; Worplesdon, West Hill and Woking. I always find the debate about which of those three lovely Surrey heathland courses is the best an amusing one. I have friends with firm favourites for each of them. In my view they are all great so I would choose six holes from each. Arguably Woking boasts some of the best holes (but in my view has a couple of weak ones).

On this occasion, after playing Scotscraig, I could remember every hole. Indeed, I could remember every shot I played and I should disclose why. I have spoken before how one's impression of a course is inevitably coloured by the way you played it. A course which you played well generally gets a good write up. Well, I had played Scotscraig once before and had enjoyed it but my memories were quite vague. On this occasion, after a sticky start, I had, for me, an excellent round playing the last 11 holes in level par, somewhat ahead of expectations for a 12-handicap golfer. I won't bore you with the detail – indeed there was nothing spectacular about it, merely an unusual lack of incompetence.

It's not a spectacular course, neither in its setting nor its design. Rather you encounter uniformly good holes in pleasant surroundings. It is perhaps not a course to be described with superlatives but certainly one with plenty of variety and interest. The changes of elevation are relatively modest but put to good effect; the routing is varied so the wind direction ever changing; dog-legs are generally subtle rather than sharp; heather, gorse and pine trees are all hazards but none dominate. Perhaps the front nine is the stronger of the two and there is a touch of parkland feel to a couple of the back nine holes but these are minor criticisms. 6 and 13 are great Par 3s, neither long but both deceptive and requiring good club selection. Perhaps the pick of the Par 4s are 7, where you need to decide whether to play short of a sharp ridge or risk a longer shot to a much tighter fairway, and 12, a relative short Par 4 requiring an accurate drive avoiding bunkers on the left and a tricky downhill second avoiding bunkers short right.

I am going to return to the topic of clubhouses as this tour has offered an interesting variety. The location of the clubhouse was very much part of the course designer's remit when commissioned to layout a completely new course.

Let's discuss the 'ideal' clubhouse. It should have a view over the course but this can mean many things. In this respect a slightly elevated position helps and the likes of Moray and Cruden Bay benefit from this though most are restricted to having views of the 1st and/or the 18th holes. There are a number of famous examples of clubhouses which overlook greens which are not the 18th – I think of Woking which overlooks the 14th green, Worplesdon, the 4th Green and Falsterbo in Sweden where from the terrace you watch players putt on the 7th green. But there are great exceptions: Royal St George's is surely one of golf's great clubhouses but you can't see any of the course from it. The same is true at Walton Heath. And maybe it is best for the clubhouse to be not too close to the course. I mentioned the rather nerve-racking experience of teeing off at Duff House Royal only a few feet from the bar and I always think the 18th green at West Hill is uncomfortably close to the terrace. The chatter from the bar can be distracting for those trying to hole a crucial putt especially if the flag is at the back of the green.

The other function that a perfect clubhouse should perform is to enable golfers to fraternise over at very least a drink with, ideally, the option of food after a round as that is for me a fundamental part of any round of golf. Too often clubs close their bars too early or only serve food at lunchtimes. It's difficult and costly but it is also a little 'chicken and egg' – like bus services: the more available the service is, the more it will be used and the scale created will make it viable.

Clubhouses should also showcase the golf club with trophy cabinets and pictures and Honours Boards of various competitions which give a flavour of the club's history. I always enjoy perusing a club's trophy cabinet with its array of silverware, some old, some not so old, some amusingly eccentric.

Perhaps my favourite is Eindhovensche, the Harry Colt course in the Netherlands which I visited in my last book. An attractive thatched building, slightly raised with a large terrace from where you can see holes 1, 9, 10 and 18 as well as a distant view of 16. It overlooks the putting green and has a large lake behind it. The clubhouse is well-designed with changing rooms below and receptions rooms above and crucially is almost always open for refreshments – for example, it serves meals until 6pm in winter and 9pm in summer. That is the clubhouse of a proper club. It is always disappointing to come off a golf course on a summer's evening at say 7pm to find that food is no longer served. In this respect it is good to see clubs franchising out catering to businesses which serve both the club and the community – Fortrose and Rosemarkie, Pitlochry and Reigate Heath are examples. If this can create the scale to enable food and drink to be served for longer hours then it can only be a good thing.

While my play on my recent visit to Scotscraig certainly helped form my favourable impression, the weather was showery on the day we played so that didn't flatter the course.

I would also say that, as with all the venues so far in this book, the welcome was friendly and the clubhouse an important part of the experience. It is always going to suffer by comparison with its more famous neighbours in St Andrews and the more scenic locations of the Fife south coast but Scotscraig should not be missed out.

A traditional revetted bunker on Musselburgh Old Links

A cask from the new Holyrood Distillery

THE LOTHIANS

'British golf was first played over links or 'green fields'. Nature was their architect and beast and man their contractors.'

Sir Guy Campbell (1885-1960)
The History of Golf in Britain

IN *OF PEATS and Putts* I included a chapter on East Lothian which I noted had a rich supply of delightful golf courses but just one whisky distillery, Glenkinchie in Pencaitland. Since then, Edinburgh has itself spawned two new whisky distilleries (with more on the way) so there is much to discuss. Edinburgh also has an inordinate number of golf courses (surely more than any other city in the world) and being the city of my birth, I would seem spoilt for choice. In truth, I have played very little golf in the city. There are the historic courses of Bruntsfield and Royal Burgess (the latter in particular boasting a magnificent clubhouse) and there are Mortonhall, Dalmahoy and Duddingston, all classy parkland offerings as well as plenty of other, less well-known, good ones. Yet only three (the first three mentioned above) generally qualify in Scotland's Top 100 and somehow, despite my love of Edinburgh, I have never found golf in the city that inspiring. Perhaps it is because within about twenty-five miles in East Lothian there are so many courses of exceptional quality. Indeed, while Edinburgh itself can only claim about three courses in Scotland's Top 100, East Lothian has many; the lovely course I chose in my last book, Kilspindie, is rated only the 10th best in the area.

Just to be contrary, though, I am going to choose a course which not only does not appear in Scotland's Top 100 but is also has only 9 holes. It does, however, hold the distinction of being one of only 14 courses in the UK which has held The Open. This course is Musselburgh Old Links. My reasons for this choice are many. It is clearly a very historic course and allows us to discuss many of the historic characters in the evolution of golf. It is also very close to Edinburgh (while it is now in East Lothian, being on the very edge of Edinburgh when it used to be in Midlothian) and is nowadays very easy to play and will support my contention that 9 hole golf should be encouraged. Perhaps, though the main reason is that I went to school over the road from the course and have happy memories of hitting a ball around it during the 1970s. The course you play today is, however, very different from then.

It cannot be said to be a location of substantial beauty. Bernard Darwin, in his famous 1910 book *The Golf Courses of the British Isles*, is rather scathing. 'The way to Musselburgh lies for the most part through factory chimneys and slag heaps, nor is the first glimpse of the course much more prepossessing than the surrounding scenery.' He states that on first impressions the course is 'rather flat and devoid of features.' While today most of the factory chimneys and slag heaps have gone, I can understand his impressions. The course is situated in the middle of Musselburgh racecourse which dates from

1815. During the 1970s, when I was at school at Loretto next door, the club had fallen into abeyance and the course had sadly been badly neglected. Most of the greens and some tees were still there and some were occasionally cut though I am not sure who did this. In truth it was not a golf course but an area of links where you could hit golf shots. But for practice and some exercise and friendly competition two minutes from school, it was a blessing. It was not until the early 1980s that the existing Musselburgh Old Links Club was formed and the course brought back into play. The racecourse has been similarly refurbished since that time.

The course has throughout its complicated history been the location of many prestigious golf clubs. Indeed in the 1870s the course was the base of not only the Honourable Company of Edinburgh Golfers (before it moved to Tom Morris designed Muirfield) but also the Royal Burgess Golfing Society of Edinburgh (before it moved to a Tom Morris designed course at Barnton in Edinburgh), The Bruntsfield Golfing Society (before it moved to a Willie Park designed course near Barnton) and The Royal Musselburgh Golf Club (before it moved to a new James Braid designed course a few miles away in Musselburgh). The course was not left without any play as at that time around fifty other clubs and golfing societies used Musselburgh links as their base. How they managed to share the modest nine holes, I am not sure. After the four big prestigious clubs left, the town council took over the running of the course but in the 20th century the course went into decline with the growth of bigger and better courses elsewhere.

The course today has been nicely restored but it cannot be argued that it is a top-class location or a magnificent test of golf. Yet, it oozes history and the holes are fun. Indeed Bernard Darwin, after his cautious initial impressions goes on to say; 'Yet if, after we have played over the course, we adhere to this our first view, we shall show ourselves to be persons of superficial minds and of little discernment.'

The debate as to whether Musselburgh or St Andrews is the oldest golf course in the world is not a very useful one as it depends on when the playing of golf on a particular piece of land allows that piece of land to become a golf course. There was golf being played in Scotland at both St Andrews and Musselburgh, and indeed elsewhere, in the 16th century but documentation exists of some form of formal play from 1672 in Musselburgh. The course was originally seven holes with an eighth hole being added in 1838 and then a ninth as late as 1870 just prior to it holding its first Open Championship in 1874. This proved to be a home win for Mungo Park, brother of Willie Park Senior, the winner of the first ever Open in 1860. Indeed, four of the six Opens held at Musselburgh were won by home players, with Bob Ferguson, David Brown and Willie Park Junior also winning on their home turf.

The 9 holes are not long, being under 3,000 yards off the back tees, but it is not that easy. There are five Par 4s, three Par 3s and one Par 5. While only one of the Par 4s is over 400 yards, two of the Par 3s are over 200 yards. It begins with a Par 3 of 240 yards which was the original 8th hole added in 1832, playing across the racecourse towards the grandstands. You need a clean full shot (a driver for me) to make it onto the elevated green. The course then heads eastwards with two relatively easy Par 4s though the approaches to the green, particularly on the second, require plenty of care. Stroke index

1 is the 4th, Mrs Forman's, a long Par 4 with a tricky drive and, depending on the pin position, an even trickier second. The green is difficult with some exaggerated swales and three putting an obvious danger. Mrs Forman's was the name of the pub which overlooks the green. It had been built in the 1820s by George Forman's father. In 1826, after he had taken over the running of the pub from his father, he married Marion Bowman who for the next six decades ran the establishment in, by all accounts, a rigorous manner so that it became known as 'Mrs Forman's'. She was famed for her Welsh Rarebit and it became a local institution for golfers who, during the 1870s and 1880s, the heyday of the course, would often stop for a refreshment mid-round. Indeed, it was at Mrs Forman's in 1870 when Old Tom Morris, playing a challenge match against his rival Willie Park Senior, walked off the course complaining that the partisan local crowd were preventing him from playing his shots properly. Sadly, just a few years ago the pub closed and the plot has been converted into housing.

The holes back generally play into the westerly wind so are tougher. The Par 3 5th is well guarded by bunkers, the 6th and Par 5 7th provide some relief with more easily accessible greens, before you reach the 240 yard (into the prevailing wind) Par 3 8th where a three feels like a birdie. 9 is then a dogleg to an awkward green. This is not top-class golfing terrain but the holes are at times deceptive and generally suit a running approach which adds to the fun.

I have to say it is a thrill to see this course and the club back in operation after having been neglected for so long. It holds a special place in Scottish golfing history, with the Parks of Musselburgh as famous as the Morris's of St Andrew's in their day. The original clubhouse, built by The Edinburgh Royal Burgess Golfing Society in 1873, was a classic late Victorian Scottish building. When the Royal Burgess Club left for Edinburgh in 1893, it fell into disrepair and during the 20th century it had a chequered history being used for a variety of purposes including as a 'dental appliances factory' which sounds slightly sinister. However, the new club, with assistance from both the Royal and Ancient Golfing Society and the local council managed to buy the building back in 1995 and restore it to its original purpose and it is now an asset to the local community as well as an important piece of golfing history. Anyone with an interest in golf's history should visit.

I found it an extraordinary fact when researching *Of Peats and Putts* that neither of Scotland's two great cities, Edinburgh and Glasgow, boasted a malt-whisky distillery. While its last malt distillery, Glen Sciennes, closed in 1925, Edinburgh had remained a centre of grain distilling with two large industrial distilleries, the Caledonian and the North British. The former, once the largest in the country, was eventually mothballed in 1988 so the latter, built in the late 19th century by Usher to provide competition to the growing DCL company, became Edinburgh's only distillery of any type over the past three decades. Today it is a joint venture between Diageo and the Edrington group so is largely a low-cost industrial producer of grain whisky for blends.

Both Edinburgh and Glasgow had a long history of distilling with Edinburgh and Leith in particular being central to the development of many of the big, blended brands. Edinburgh was the headquarters in 1877 of the newly formed DCL, the Distillers Company Limited, created by the amalgamation of five Lowland patent-still grain distillers, which has been the central player in the industry ever since and morphed over the years into today's Diageo. Yet, since the early 20th century the industry had largely moved its centre of gravity to the north and the western isles. However, now Glasgow has two new malt distilleries and Edinburgh three. This points to not just the new health of the industry but the role of whisky distilleries in tourism as they all have successful visitor centres. Another representation of the growth of whisky tourism is the opening by Diageo of the Johnnie Walker Experience in Princes Street in Edinburgh. Diageo was encouraged by the success of its Guinness Brewery Visitor Centre in Dublin. It makes a lot of sense to convert a retail site in the centre of a city attracting international tourists into a promotional vehicle for an international brand. However, the Guinness tour takes place at the Guinness Brewery while this one is in a converted department store and the effect is rather more contrived. It is well worth a visit nonetheless and includes two rooftop bars and restaurants with fine views over the centre of Edinburgh. If you are wanting to be a real whisky tourist you can now also stay at a new, smart hotel called 'The Angel's Share' just around the corner.

Apart from the opening of new distilleries, one other Edinburgh based whisky business is worth mentioning. The Scotch Malt Whisky Society was founded in Leith in 1983, then owned by Glenmorangie from 2003, and now operates from its headquarters in Queen Street. In 2015 it was sold to a group of private investors. It has nearly 30,000 subscriber members, over half from overseas, and specialises in buying and bottling single casks from distilleries all over Scotland.

They also operate member bars in Edinburgh, Glasgow and London as well as 'Partner Bars' in 30 different countries. In 2021 the business floated on the AIM market under the holding company Artisanal Spirits. It shows the international appeal of Scotch malt whisky and that opening a new distillery is not the only business model which can leverage the global market potential.

The first new malt to be distilled in Edinburgh was actually by John Crabbie & Company, a subsidiary of the Liverpool based private drinks group Halewood International, which has since also acquired whisk(e)y interests in both Wales and Ireland. An English whisky distillery is also planned for Blackpool – ideal to go with a visit to Royal Lytham and St. Annes! The brand's history goes back some two hundred years as a merchant and blender of whisky. While it operated a grain distillery in Haddington for a while during the mid-19th century it became better known for the production of fruit cordials, and Crabbie's Green Ginger Wine became the brand's iconic product. This has strong golfing associations as a 'Whisky Mac' (ginger wine and whisky) is a popular drink before embarking on a round of golf on a cold winter morning. John Crabbie was also a co-founder of the original North British grain distillery. Crabbies was acquired by DCL in the 1960s who then sold it to McDonald Muir, then owners of Glenmorangie in the 1980s, before Halewood bought the brand in 2007. As well as using the brand to market alcoholic ginger beer, they have now revived the whisky brand and the new Bonnington distillery will give the brand its own production. However, it was a small pilot distillery in Granton which produced Edinburgh's first malt spirit in 2018 while the new distillery was being constructed. This beat the first distillation at the new Holyrood distillery in the summer of 2019. Meanwhile, a third distillery, the Port of Leith distillery is under construction next to the Royal Yacht Britannia in Leith Dock. Suddenly Edinburgh has become a destination for whisky lovers and, recognising the tourism potential, the owners of each are contemplating marketing an Edinburgh 'whisky trail'.

**The distinctively-shaped small
still at the Holyrood Distillery**

All the distilleries have interesting stories but I have decided to feature the Holyrood Distillery as it is a good example of a new Scottish start-up using a combination of Scottish and international funding and experience. The co-founders are David Robertson, an ex-master distiller at Macallan and a Canadian couple, Kelly and Rob Carpenter (Rob was the founder of the Canadian branch of the Scotch Malt Whisky Society), along with a number of other investors. They have converted an old, listed railway engine shed dating from the 1830s which sits in a quiet location in the shadow of Arthur's Seat on the edge of Holyrood Park. A smart shop and visitor centre has been included while they are also selling gin and maturing spirit to generate cash while they wait for their whisky to mature. The equipment is modern, a one-tonne semi-lauter mash tun and six 5,000 litre washbacks while the stills are particularly tall for their size with descending lyne arms. Overall capacity is a modest 250,000 litres. I am not going to go into the details of how this equipment is designed to produce a certain type of spirit as it is too technical for this book and I don't pretend to understand fully. Indeed, my only observation is that Macallan, from where David Robertson hailed, boasts of small squat stills while these being relatively tall tend towards the Glenmorangie principle. However, it is not the equipment which the owners are suggesting will produce their unique proposition but the use of specific mash bills (recipes of malted barley and yeast) to deliver different flavours. Holyrood is looking to learn from Edinburgh's strong historical associations with beer brewing to experiment with different barley varieties – they are working with Heriot Watt University to research whether heritage barley varieties can produce distinct flavours - and malting processes such as chocolate malt, toasted malt and roasted malt as well as trying a range of yeast types, including more traditional brewing yeasts rather than distilling ones. Many of these variables are represented in bottles of four different new-make spirits which they have made available for sale. Each outline on the label the precise make-up of the recipes as well as the fermentation time. These are called 'Made by Edinburgh', 'Crystal Malt', 'Brewers x Distillers Yeast' and 'Chocolate Malt'. All these varieties are being introduced before looking at different maturation policies based on cask size and type from new oak, ex-bourbon, sherry and wine casks. No wonder no two whiskies are the same.

All the above is explained in the tour which contains generous amounts of tasting opportunities and you can engage as much or as little as you like in the detail. My overall impression was that this is another professional start-up and it will undoubtedly produce a high-quality, interesting product. The extent to which this product will be very different, I don't know. It is commonly believed that most of the final influence on flavour comes from the maturation so will these recipe tweaks still be noticeable after five years in a cask? To my mind what is good is that, despite the tight regulations governing the production of Scotch whisky, there is always a new angle to investigate, a new approach, be it to recipe or to process, to explore. Complexity, diversity, heterogeneity: call it what you like, it is what makes whisky so fascinating and it is encouraging to see new whisky businesses innovating in this way.

As an amateur enthusiast and not being a chemist, it never ceases to amaze me how many different factors are involved in delivering a particular tasting whisky. I have listened over the years to experts discussing everything from the varieties of malted barley to the significance of different yeasts, from the length of fermentation to the importance of the precise nature of the distilling including the design and shape of the stills and how the spirit is cut. Then there is another whole conversation to be had on maturation: origin of oak, time, temperature and sherry or wine barrel finishes etc. etc. What it proves is that there is no perfect answer. I have found a similar drink to which this applies: coffee. When I was still working, one of the most important factors in making a cup of coffee at home was speed. I needed a shot in the morning before going to work so a pod machine provided the answer. After retiring, and particularly during the first UK lockdown, I decided that as speed was no longer an important criterion, I would look to make myself the best coffee possible. I bought a machine and trained myself to be a barista! Every day I would be able to make the perfect cup of coffee. How wrong could I be?

Several years on from doing this I am drinking some nice coffee but every day is a surprise – a bit like my golf, the results are quite variable. Only now do I realise that there are so many factors involved even when I am supposedly using a good machine. First, the ingredients; I now buy special roasted coffee and not just stuff from the supermarket. I am beginning to find the ones I like, not dark roast bitter ones but milder roasted, yet strong and earthy ones. I was persuaded that buying beans and grinding yourself was the best way to get a fresh flavour. But to make an espresso or an americano you need to get the right setting on the grinder. Just when you think you have conquered that you find that different beans grind in different ways so the right setting for one bean may not be the right one for another which shatters more easily! How hard to tamp? Not too much but not too little. I now filter the water which is necessary for hard Oxfordshire water but not required when I'm in Cornwall. What is the best temperature to set the machine at? Certainly not too hot as this will damage the flavour.

Yet, even now every day is different. Some days I do produce an excellent cup of coffee and feel extremely pleased with myself. The next day I ostensibly make it in exactly the same way and yet it doesn't taste quite the same. This corroborates my theory about whisky tasting: that context is an enormous factor in how you react to the product. With my coffee, I realise that I have to concentrate very hard to produce exactly the right coffee day in and day out but in fact it won't taste the same every day because every day I feel a bit different and will react in a slightly different way. The same is true with both the making and tasting of whisky as it is with the playing of golf: no two ex-bourbon or sherry casks will produce exactly the same maturation effect; exactly the same shot hit will not always produce exactly the same result as a tiny difference in the wind will mean it will bounce in a slightly different spot and react in potentially a very different way. This is why I think that an overly scientific approach to the golf swing or golf equipment technology is not for me – the beauty of golf and whisky lies in unpredictable variety.

The four stills at the Borders Distillery are named after
the founders; George, Tony, George and Tim

The view from the 14th tee at The Roxburghe with the
Victorian viaduct over the River Tweed in the background

THE BORDERS

'We look to Scotland for all our ideas of civilisation.'

Voltaire (1694-1778)

French philosopher and historian

WHEN I WROTE my first book on Scotland, I never considered including a chapter on the Borders despite it being where I was brought up as a child. There were no whisky distilleries and in truth the golf courses, though many in number, were not among the best on offer in Scotland. The region is best described as that south of Edinburgh and to the east of the M74 motorway from Carlisle to Glasgow and it is a region with its own distinctive look and culture. Unlike the central belt of Scotland, it is largely rural, comprising only small towns and villages. Yet, unlike the Highlands, the landscape is hilly rather than mountainous. I lived near Melrose on the River Tweed in the heart of the Borders, a pretty, small town of around 2-3,000 people depending on which of the many neighbouring villages you included. Rather like South Wales, the major sport was rugby, and in the amateur days, when I was a child, local derby rugby matches would attract several thousand supporters – a relatively high proportion of the local population. Melrose has the fame of having invented Rugby Sevens (a local butcher called Ned Haig is usually given the credit) and the Melrose Sevens Tournament has taken place on the second Saturday in April for over 100 years. In its heyday up to 15,000 spectators from all over Scotland would descend on this small, quiet town to enjoy the spectacle which would attract teams from all over the world. Guest teams from Australia and South Africa were regularly invited. Golf was also a popular sport with most towns having a small course. I played mainly at two local courses, both very scenic; Melrose, on the slopes of the Eildon Hills, and Torwoodlee, just north of Galashiels on the banks of the Tweed. Golf here was very much a leisure pursuit, certainly not taken as seriously as rugby. Many of the courses are 9 holes including Innerleithen which is one of the oldest, the first course to be designed by Willie Park Junior, of Sunningdale fame. All these courses are enjoyable places to play but none can claim to be top class venues; many Borderers wanting a proper test of golf would be members of clubs in East Lothian, only about an hour's drive away.

This changed in 1977 when Dave Thomas designed a course on land owned by the Duke of Roxburghe along the banks of the River Teviot between Kelso and Jedburgh. There was also a luxury hotel and restaurant which pre-dated the course. It is perhaps an unusual choice for me as in 2018 it was bought by a German property developer and is now called, rather strangely, Schloss Roxburghe, so is very much a corporate and luxury venue though the course also hosts a local club. However, it is a very good layout, is the only course in the Borders to be ranked in the Top 100 in Scotland and the green fees are extremely reasonable for a course of this quality.

Distilling has also undergone a revival in the Borders. It was never an important area for whisky distilling; tweed and knitwear manufacturing being the main local industries. My father owned a Tweed mill in Selkirk with his business partner. One connection with distilling is that arguably the oldest name in distilling, Haig, originated in the Borders. The Haig family home was at Bemersyde a few miles from Melrose where I was brought up. What distilling which did take place was in the southern area with two distilleries near Langholm which closed in the early 20th century. There is also some evidence of a small distillery which operated in Hawick in the early 19th century but, by all accounts, it was short-lived. Hawick, however, is the location for the first new distillery to operate in the Borders for over one hundred years, aptly named The Borders Distillery. Since it began production in 2018 there have been a number of other ventures announced: the Reivers Distillery owned by Mossburn (who also operate the new Torabhaig distillery on Skye which I will visit in my next book) is planned at a site near Melrose while, more recently, Jackson Distillers have announced a £46 million investment in a huge grain distillery in nearby St Boswells. Finally, Dark Sky Spirits, began building a small malt distillery just outside Moffatt. Suddenly, the Borders has more distilleries than Campbeltown.

As a Melrose man, perhaps I shouldn't be choosing the Borders Distillery in Hawick to feature - in rugby circles, Hawick was Melrose's fierce local rival - but it is undoubtedly the pioneer and has quickly developed a strong reputation. It was founded by four ex-colleagues from William Grant & Sons, so there is no shortage of whisky knowledge and experience. They formed The Three Stills Company and raised capital in conjunction with a small private equity company to renovate an old brownfield site in the middle of Hawick and build the Borders Distillery. The buildings date from Victorian times and have always been part of Hawick's industrial heritage, being at various times a sweetie factory (home of the famous *Hawick Balls* – a hard mint which I remember from my childhood) and an engineering company. They have been beautifully restored and won a local buildings design award, and the location next to the River Teviot and above an underground loch provides a ready water source. I noticed that the four stills were named after the founders: George, Tony, John and Tim. The equipment (mash-tun, eight stainless steel washbacks and four stills) was all supplied by Forsyths.

Production began in 2018 as did sales of four products: a blend called Clan Fraser, targeted in particular at the African market, a blended malt called Lower East Side (clearly these two whiskies were distilled elsewhere) as well as Kerr's Borders Gin and Puffing Billy Vodka, both produced in the new distillery. These latter two products are premium ones, made with local malted barley and, for the gin, the spirit redistilled using a Carterhead still, where the botanicals are steamed in a basket during distillation, while the vodka is steamed through charcoal rather than filtered as a liquid. The latter is certainly unique which together with the use of barley gives the product a distinctive taste and texture.

There are regular tours which are all hosted not by specialist 'tour guides' but by the distillers themselves making the experience more personal. The distilling process is fairly familiar: they use a yeast called Pinnacle-M (sounds like a golf ball) and the fermentation time is approximately 80 hours. At the time of writing, the malt whisky has not been released so we don't know a lot about the brand or the product and what their approach to maturing will be. The proposition, however, as with many of the new start-ups, is a sustainable one using local barley from just twelve farms within 30 miles of the distillery, from Newcastleton in the south of the region to near St Abbs in the north. All organic by-product is returned to two farms where it is used, amongst other things, to grow tomatoes. It is good to see a town, which has suffered some hard times with the decline of the textile industry, benefit from an exciting new business. Perhaps this can be the case for the Borders as a whole – whisky replacing textiles as a long term, sustainable industry supporting the local economy.

The Roxburghe is only a few miles away further down the River Teviot between Jedburgh and Kelso. I hadn't played the course for many years so was keen to return. The new investment is immediately apparent with a large new building being erected alongside the old house and overlooking the first fairway. There is a small, modern clubhouse which supports the local members' club.

The Roxburghe is quite a classy course and there are many well-designed holes. I will mention a few: the second is a fairly benign Par 4 with a large fairway bunker and an appealing downhill second shot to the green. The fourth, the first Par 3, is over water and depending on the pin position can be challenging. My first attempt was wet but I decided to take three off the tee rather than drop by the hazard and enjoyed hitting it over the flag to about six feet. The fifth is a snaky Par 5 with many subtle changes in elevation. Just before and after the turn there are more dramatic elevation changes with the sharply downhill Par 3 8th followed by a climb back up the hill to the 9th. 10 then falls precipitously back down the hill only for 11 to take you back up. It's quite a walk. 14 is the hole often featured in photographs as you tee off from on high and the Par 5 proceeds along the banks of the River Tweed with the iconic railway viaduct in the background. While visually pleasing, it is in truth not a great golf hole. A steeply uphill Par 3 follows and then three more Par 4s to finish, perhaps the blind 17th being the best where the second shot down to a raised green can be a little scary.

The quirky downhill Par 3 finishing hole at Selkirk

I have to share with you a moment on 18. We all have shots which we remember and, as professional sportsmen would say, provide 'positives' to take away from a mediocre round.

Mediocre was perhaps a generous description of my golf on that day – mainly indifferent shot-making with sporadic outbreaks of competence. The 18th is an uphill drive with a slight dogleg left and a bunker on the corner. It was clearly too far for me to carry, so it was the one hazard I needed to avoid. I didn't avoid it and, to rub salt into the wound, my lie was impossible, right up against the face. My only option was to drop it back in the middle of the bunker with a one-shot penalty. From there, I hit the ball out but remained still nearly 200 yards from the flag having played three. What a disappointing end to a disappointing round. I got out my rescue club but then decided that the wind was freshening and it was uphill so I decided to change to a gentle three wood. I connected cleanly and the ball never left the line of the flag landing on the green and rolling up just four inches short. I should have given it a little more…

It is amazing the difference your final shot can make. And there is something special about a perfectly hit three wood – more so than any other club for some reason especially when you are going for the green. So, I came off the Roxburghe in good spirits and enjoyed an excellent supper in the smart hotel bar, something I would strongly recommend.

The Roxburghe is a fine golf course yet somehow it doesn't stir the emotions. It is not bland as the design is high quality with a range of hole types and the countryside and the views are delightful. It is probably because the land is not obvious golfing landscape. The soil is agricultural rather than sandy (I guess that it gets quite wet in winter) and in order to carve 18 well-designed holes, there are some very long walks between holes, something I am not keen on.

I think the issue is that this is not natural golfing terrain. I believe that some of the best golf courses don't look like golf courses. In this way they achieve what many of the early designers sought in being naturally sympathetic to their surroundings. I remember taking my son to The Open at Muirfield in 2002 – he would have been about 12 years old. He had heard me talking about Muirfield being one of the greatest courses and his impression of great golf courses was gained from television coverage of tournaments such as the Masters. Walking through the gates into Muirfield, you could see the stands and the great tented village which impressed him but when we walked out into the centre of the course he said 'is this it?' Like many links courses, there is not much golf course to see. You have an area of natural linksland through which a golf course has been constructed in a very understated way. The same can be said at, for example, Westward Ho! or indeed some heathland courses such as Hankley Common where the vastness of the heathland common dwarfs the golf course which has been built within it. This appeals to me from both an aesthetic and an environmental perspective. And this is the debate about many new links courses. The controversy over the Coul Links project at Embo north of Dornoch speaks to this. The proposal was to build in an area of Special Scientific Interest and was appalling to many. Yet, sympathetically done, a marrying of a new course with the local environment can be achieved and the proposal by Coore and Crenshaw was very focused on this. Indeed, a golf course can help look after a natural landscape because even some natural landscapes need managing. The Roxburghe is not unsympathetic to its surroundings but it is also not natural. Perhaps all it is lacking is about 100 years of history.

However, I think it is more than that. The course is well-designed, the environment is extremely pretty (the course may not have been there for 100 years but many of the trees have) and the course is kept in excellent condition. So why is it not a course that I would like to play every week? It is about the soil; the soil is not conducive to playing a running game so there is a much greater level of 'target golf' and if you are playing 'target golf', many design features are irrelevant. If all you are calculating is how far you need to fly the ball in the air, you are removing one of main variables of the game: how the ball will bounce. You are removing much of the fun of golf.

I am therefore going to do what I did with distilleries in my final chapter of *Of Peats and Putts* and with golf courses in my final chapter of *Mashies and Mash-Tuns* when I agonised, rather pointlessly, about whether to feature Tralee or Dingle. I am going to give you another course to complete your Borders golfing experience – not either of the two courses of my childhood but a third nearby which I always remember enjoying and which, with hindsight, introduced me to the type of golf I like best. While Innerleithen was Willie Park Junior's first design, Selkirk was one of his last, designed on his return from the United States in 1924, the year before he died. Selkirk is the only true heathland course in the Borders and while by no measure a great course, it is in many ways a 'classic' as it very much requires you to play 'the running game' and the stunning scenery definitely provides a 'joy to be alive feeling'. It also fits naturally into its surroundings in the Border hills. At just 2,800 yards off the back tees, it is short and the structure of holes is hardly ideal, starting with five Par 4s and ending with three Par 3s interrupted by the Par 5 8th. The 8th is probably the best hole both scenically and in golfing terms, over 500 yards in length and requiring much thought with the second shot needing to find a good spot from which to approach the hidden green with your third. From the first hole, a modest downhill 380-yard Par 4, you realise that it is the control of your shots to the green which is the challenge. But surely that is the main challenge of golf, not the ability to drive the ball 300 yards?

I played it in early May after a cold April and the condition of the course was not great. I think that the course would benefit from some work on its grasses but this is a small club with limited resources. I must return in the summer to judge how it plays in drier conditions. The greens were exceptionally slow but in early spring I can accept this. Lots of people complain about greens being slow but there are many occasions when this makes sense: in wet winter conditions, in exceptionally hot summer conditions and on very exposed links courses during high winds, leaving a good growth of grass on greens makes sense. The golfer should adapt which is why my one pre-round routine (I'm not one for hitting 50 balls on the range before embarking on a round) is to take a few putts on the practice green and get a feel for its pace. My only complaint is when the putting green bears no relation to those on the course which can happen; indeed, I don't think I mentioned, this would have been my one complaint about Hopeman.

The drive at the 1st is blind and somewhat intimidating as it disappears over the brow of the hill whence it falls sharply down towards the green. The drive needs to be well-controlled and your second requires careful judgement. The second hole is a short Par 4 but this time the blind tee shot is uphill with a bit more room. The third drive sets up well into the neck of a hill where you play your second uphill towards a green at the top. The 4th is not dissimilar, back the way, while 5 requires a long raking fade, again carefully controlled. The green is a small target nestling at the foot of the hill. While the Par 3 6th is not a great golf hole, played dramatically uphill to a flat green, it is fun, and the next is a very tough longer Par 3 where you need to favour the left. As I said, the 8th is an excellent par 5, a long curling valley fairway at the top of the hill reaching a generous but hidden green. The 9th sits high on the hill above the clubhouse and you play down to the green below; the inverse of the short 6th. It is about 30 yards longer than the 6th but probably requires at least two clubs less. As I think Wayne Riley once said, a distance device is 'as much use as an ashtray on a motorbike.'

I have decided to include Selkirk in this book as it also serves as a precursor for my next episode, the third 9 in what has become my *Of Peats and Putts* Scottish trilogy. The courses I have chosen for episode three include a number of 9-holers and none appear in the Top 80 courses in Scotland (two sneak into the Top 100). They are chosen for their enjoyment more than their technical golfing quality. If you go to the Borders, the Roxburghe is the best course and you should visit it and you will enjoy it. But on balance, the 18th at the Roxburghe excepted, I think I enjoyed the experience of Selkirk more.

The Borders Distillery, as with Arbikie, Lindores Abbey and Holyrood, is also a model for the distilleries I want to visit – new start-ups which will create a new sector in an already thriving industry. It is remarkable how many there are and fascinating to observe how they are all finding a particular angle to promote.

Afterword

'...it is of vital importance to avoid anything that tends to make the game simple or stereotyped. On the contrary, every endeavour should be made to increase its strategy, variety, mystery, charm and elusiveness so that we shall never get bored with it, but continue to pursue it with increasing zest...'

Dr Alister Mackenzie (1870-1934)
The Spirit of St Andrews

LIFE IS COMPLICATED; golf and whisky are too. It is the complexity of golf and whisky which make them so appealing, therefore, equally, it is right to embrace positively the complexities of life. I remember a character in the William Boyd novel, *Love is Blind,* who reflects: 'I always think a life without complications isn't really a life, you know. In life things go wrong, nothing stays the same and there's nothing you can do about it. Friends betray you, family is a nightmare, lovers are fickle. This is the norm, no? What kind of world would it be where nothing ever went wrong, where everything stayed the same, life followed its designated path – family was adorable, friends and lovers were faithful and true? You know, I don't think I'd like that kind of world. We're made for complications, we human beings.' The same could be said for a round of golf and the making of a good malt whisky.

I have said before that it is the glorious uncertainty and unpredictability of both golf and whisky which make them so appealing. If we knew that from 100 yards we could always hit an easy straight shot close to the flag, golf would become boring. Sometimes we don't; we pull it, shank it, top it or just fluff it. It's annoying, frustrating, maddening. But that is partly why we enjoy it because if we didn't occasionally pull it, shank it, top it or fluff it, the satisfaction of when we hit it to 3 feet would not be the same. Whisky too. To use a fashionable term, they are both diverse and in many ways.

Golf also has its share of mysteries. How many of the following can you relate to: how many times have you lost your ball, placed your bag down in the rough, spent three minutes looking for it before returning to your bag to find the ball lying next to it? Do you find a short two-foot putt with a bit of borrow much easier than a totally straight one? How come all my provisional drives off the tee go straight down the middle? And sometimes do you stand over a ten-foot putt and know that you are going to hole it while on the next hole you stand over a seemingly straightforward two-foot putt and know that you are going to miss it?

Whisky's mysteries are perhaps more subtle. You put new-make spirit, distilled from the same batch, on the same day, into two ex-bourbon barrels which sit in a warehouse next to each other for five years: will the resulting whisky in each barrel taste exactly the same? Not necessarily. We know that a malt whisky to which a drop of water is added will taste different – there is science to explain why it will – but taste is something very personal and very prone to the influence of context.

It is some five years since I completed *Of Peats and Putts* my first book examining whisky and golf in Scotland and much has happened both in the world at large and in the narrow context of whisky and golf in Scotland. Looking back at my conclusions, I suggested that the whisky industry looked to be in good health but I worried a little about golf: declining club membership, a slightly stuffy and elitist image in some areas, the fact that it takes a long time to play in our new time-poor age, all being issues which needed addressing.

I was right about whisky. Despite the challenges of Covid, a trade war with the United States which temporarily increased tariffs, Brexit, the cost-of-living crisis, the industry seems to be going from strength to strength whether you judge it by the significant investments being made by the multinationals, the purchase of distillery assets by luxury brand conglomerates or the number of entrepreneurial start-ups. The market seems to be thriving and ever diversifying and that is healthy.

Dare I say it, but I think golf is also now in better shape having undergone something of a recovery. To some extent Covid has helped it because many people have come to appreciate the benefits of regular outdoor exercise and companionship which membership of a golf club can offer. Certainly, many clubs, which were struggling with membership numbers, have filled up since the pandemic. And if this includes more women golfers and juniors, which seems generally to be the case, all the better. This, however, should not mean that more people play golf at just their own club. Quite the contrary, it should encourage more people to play at other clubs and here the role of club 'Opens', as I played in at Duff House Royal and Montrose, are very important. The more of these there are the better: Men's Opens, Women's Opens, Junior Opens, Mixed Pairs Opens, Foursomes Opens, the more variety the better. Club members experiencing other clubs and clubhouses, meeting other golfers, broadening their golfing horizons. And, as I continue to contend, with golf being a metaphor for life itself, broadening your golfing horizons will broaden your life's experience.

I also think that there is some momentum in our understanding of what makes a good golfing experience. The building of many new courses in the 1970s and 1980s in rather unsuitable locations on the 'wrong' type of soil (I have to suggest that The Roxburghe is an example of this) introduced many players to a game somewhat different from that envisaged by the likes of Old Tom Morris. Course designs became rather contrived with man-made elevations and water hazards often a feature as opposed to relying upon the natural contours of the land. With technology increasing the distance the ball could be hit, longer courses were seen as good courses. I think this is changing. While all courses have to adapt to some extent to accommodate the greater distances that the ball is being hit, simply lengthening a course does not make it 'better' or indeed more difficult. It is about the course conditions, the set-up of the greens and the run-off areas, the positioning of bunkers not just to catch bad shots but to tempt good players to take risks. Strategic designs on natural golfing terrain, which use the natural contours of the land, are becoming the norm for new courses and these same principles are being followed in the upgrade of old courses.

There has in my view been one very negative development and that is the cost of golf. Many of the famous Open courses now charge around £300 for a round and there have been significant price increases at nearly all courses. I remember playing Troon in 1998; for £100 we played a round on the Championship, a round on the Portland and a snack lunch was included. Inflation since then would suggest that this would now be around £200 but, in actual fact, the same deal today would be nearer £400. A few years ago, you could still play many high-quality courses in Scotland for around £100 but this is increasingly difficult. Indeed, I have heard clubs say that when they increased their Green Fees above £100 they got more visitors because it gave the impression that they were a better course. As in any market there is supply and demand and if clubs can sustain visitor numbers at these high prices then good luck to them; they can use the proceeds to invest in their club and their course. Fortunately, in Scotland there are so many good courses that you still don't need to pay these sums and increasingly I am enjoying seeking new 'hidden gems' where the overall experience is just as good as a day on an Open Championship venue.

The increasing premium being charged for whisky is in my view a good thing. There is also in some cases a reverse market price ratio; a special edition whisky needs to sell at a premium price to signal that it is special. Distilleries and whisky brands can offer various price tiers; this is more difficult for golf courses though in some respects 'twilight tickets' can do this.

I started this *Afterword* with a quotation from Alister MacKenzie's seminal work *The Spirit of St Andrews* which neatly sums up my contention that golf's main attraction lies in its familiar unpredictability and I will end with another quotation from this remarkable book which espouses golf as an activity which promotes health and happiness:

'One of the reasons why I, a medical man, decided to give up medicine and take to golf architecture was my firm conviction of the extraordinary influence on health of pleasurable excitement, especially when combined with fresh air and exercise.'

This serves as a perfect invitation to join me on the final leg of my Scottish odyssey to the wild west coast where we will encounter an extraordinary variety of golf courses and (mainly) new distilleries which epitomise the joys of golfing in different locations and the incredible diversity of new whisky offerings in Scotland. The locations will guarantee 'fresh air and exercise' and all deliver 'pleasurable excitement', just what the Doctor MacKenzie ordered.

About the author

ANDREW BROWN WAS born in Edinburgh, brought up in the Borders and educated at Loretto School in Musselburgh. After reading history at Cambridge University, he pursued a career in the food industry, marketing many famous brands such as Bisto, Hovis and Mr Kipling. He has three grown-up children, is now retired and, outside of his regular visits to Scotland, lives in Oxfordshire and Cornwall. Apart from playing golf he is an enthusiastic dog walker, a very average tennis player and a novice gardener.

Bibliography

While there are numerous fine books on both whisky and golf
the following were particularly relevant to this book

Malt Whisky — Charles MacLean — **Lomond Books 2013**

Scotch Whisky Its Past and Present — David Daiches — **André Deutsch 1969**

Maclean's Miscellany of Whisky — Charles MacLean — **Little Books Ltd. 2015**

Scotch Missed — Brian Townsend — **The Angels' Share 2017**

Malt Whisky Yearbook 2023 — **MagDig Media 2022**

Whisky — Aeneas Macdonald — **Birlinn 2016**

A Field Guide to Whisky — Hans Offringa — **Artisan 2017**

A Sense of Place Dave — Broom Mitchell — **Beazley 2022**

The Links — Robert Hunter — **Coventry House 2018**

Methods of early golf architecture H.S Colt and A. W. Tillinghast — *The selected writings of Alister MacKenzie,* **Coventry House Publishing 2013**

The Spirit of St Andrews — Alister MacKenzie — **Broadway Books**

Made in United States
North Haven, CT
07 August 2024

55797711R00083